Mechademia : Second Arc

Mechademia: Second Arc (ISSN 1934-2489) is published twice a year in the spring and fall by the University of Minnesota Press, 111 Third Avenue South, Suite 290, Minneapolis, MN 55401-2520. http://www.upress.umn.edu

Postmaster: Send address changes to *Mechademia: Second Arc*, University of Minnesota Press, 111 Third Avenue South, Suite 290, Minneapolis, MN 55401-2520.

All submissions must be between 5000–6000 words. Essays that are substantially longer cannot be accepted. Citations should follow the *Chicago Manual of Style*, 17th ed., using bibliographic endnotes rather than footnotes or in-text citations. Please also see the *Mechademia* Style Guide (see PDF on mechademia.net) for more details on citation style and essay formatting. Submissions and editorial queries should be sent to submissions@mechademia.net.

Books for review should be addressed to

Forrest Greenwood
Indiana University Innovation Center
2719 E 10th Street
Bloomington, IN 47408

Brian White
#101 Etosu O2, 26-14
Edogawa-ku, Shinozaki-machi 4-chome
Tokyo
Japan

Address subscription orders, changes of address, and business correspondence (including requests for permission and advertising orders) to *Mechademia: Second Arc,* University of Minnesota Press, 111 Third Avenue South, Suite 290, Minneapolis, MN 55401-2520.

Subscriptions: Regular rate.s, U.S.: individual, 1 year, $44; libraries, 1 year, $87. Outside the U.S. add $5 for each year's subscription. Checks should be made payable to the University of Minnesota Press. Back issues are $21.50 for individuals, $21.50 for libraries (plus $6 shipping for the first copy, $1.25 for each additional copy inside the U.S.; $9.50 shipping for the first copy, $6 for each additional copy, outside the U.S.). *Mechademia: Second Arc* is available online through the JSTOR Current Scholarship Program at http://jstor.org/r/umnpress.

Mechademia : Second Arc

VOLUME 12, NO. 1

FALL 2019

TRANSNATIONAL FANDOM

1 Introduction: Media Scholarship in the Contact Zone
ANDREA HORBINSKI

11 What You Watch Is What You Are?
Early Anime and Manga Fandom in the United States
ANDREA HORBINSKI

31 The Genesis of the Otaku Phenomenon in Spain:
A Journey through Fanzines, Associations, and Conventions
during the 1990s
SALOMÓN DONCEL-MORIANO URBANO

57 Subtitle and Distribute:
The Mediation Policies of Brazilian Fansubbers in Digital Networks
KRYSTAL URBANO

77 Japanese Exceptionalism and Play Hegemony: The Construction of
Ludic Traditions in Video Games Criticism
TOMÁS GRAU

96 Disrupting Centers of Transcultural Materialities: The
Transnationalization of Japan Cool through Philippine Fan Works
KRISTINE MICHELLE L. SANTOS

118 In Front of the Law: The Production and Distribution of Boys' Love
Dôjinshi in Indonesia
NICE HUANG

136 (Trans)Cultural Legibility and Online *Yuri!!! on Ice* Fandom
LORI MORIMOTO

Introduction

Media Scholarship in the Contact Zone

Bringing two fields into conversation with one another is no easy task. This issue of *Mechademia: Second Arc*, "Transnational Fandom," seeks to bridge the young, interdisciplinary field of fan studies with the established, institutionalized field of Asian studies. In the current era, in which the humanities are under siege across the globe even as the interconnectivity of the internet is threatened by political and regulatory constraints in the so-called advanced industrial countries, these conversations are more urgent than ever: if we do not hang together, assuredly we shall all hang separately. Moreover, using the strengths and weaknesses of one field to highlight the potentials and biases in the other should enable scholars working in the zones where they intersect, such as the authors in this volume, to wield both as necessary in forging a path forward in both disciplines. Where we go from here will be decided by all of us.

"Transnational fandom" is on one level redundant and on another a term that needs some explication. For those who, like me, have been embedded in online fan cultures from the 1990s onward, the idea that fandom has always been transnational is self-evident, a conclusion that research into fandom history has consistently supported. My own fan history over the past two decades spans sites such as LiveJournal, Dreamwidth, Twitter, and Tumblr, as well as volunteering with the fan advocacy nonprofit Organization for Transformative Works. Across all of these platforms, I made connections with fellow fans who spanned languages and continents from South America to Europe to Asia and Australia. These relationships were and are primarily digitally mediated, and many of them were anchored in the practices of "convergence culture," as Henry Jenkins dubbed it in his groundbreaking 2006 study of the same name.[1] What Jenkins called "transmedia" was already known to practitioners and media theorists working in Japan as the anime media mix, the powerhouse of the Japanese contents industry in which fan practices and cultures play a vital part. The young field of fan studies, which was in large part founded by scholars from the previous generation of fans—those who made the transition from offline to online fandom as adults—has in many ways taken the transnational nature of fandom as axiomatic, even if individual studies have broken fans into discrete (and more easily researchable) tranches based on specific characteristics ranging from fandom objects to gender to nationality or language.

As scholars have turned their focus on the pre-internet era, however, national boundaries have appeared to reassert themselves as particularly salient in determining fandom and its limits, especially in terms of language and political geography. For nearly two decades, the guiding star for discussions of fandom in Japanese studies has been sociologist Koichi Iwabuchi's *Recentering Globalization* (2002), in which he argued that Japanese contents industry companies were seeking to promote their media exports abroad by constructing their products (Iwabuchi's prime examples were "animations" and video games) as "culturally odorless" (*mukokuseki*).[2] Although Iwabuchi's findings, based on his fieldwork interviews with contents industry professionals, were primarily couched in terms of Japanese exports to the rest of Asia, they have been taken to apply globally in Japan studies ever since.

The only problem with applying Iwabuchi's argument in such a broad fashion is that, for those of us who remember fandom in the 1990s in Anglophone countries, it does not pass the smell test. Specifically, the idea that people who became anime fans in this decade, after anime fandom had made a definitive break from science fiction fandom in the Anglophone sphere, did not know that we were consuming Japanese media or that we were not interested in the aspects of Japanese culture displayed in the media we loved, is simply not accurate. In the United States and related Anglophone anime fandom, the 1990s were the era of "flipped manga" controversies and the "subs versus dubs" wars as a fandom legitimacy test, to say nothing of endless arguments about whether and how to translate honorifics and sound effects. On the video game side, the continuing discourse about "JRPGs" re-inscribed even fantastical "MMORPGs" like the *Final Fantasy* series within a paradigm of cultural provenance despite, as Iwabuchi recounts, their deliberate lack of cultural specificity. For all these media, moreover, the best, most coveted merchandise was always made in Japan (or in many cases, made in China and imported from Japan). We knew that we were consuming Japanese media, and we were fascinated by the image of Japan that those media presented. I was by no means unique in my generation when I studied Japanese in college based on my love for anime, a path that ultimately led to my sitting here writing this introduction.

The fan studies perspective, which attempts to take a bottom-up rather than top-down approach by focusing on audiences rather than professional creators, might have helped Iwabuchi understand that whatever industry employees in Tokyo thought they were doing, fan reactions and interpretations around the world escaped their attempts to assert control, with a lot of assistance from the internet and the networks it enabled. Fan studies recognizes that audiences are not simply passive consumers or cultural "dupes" but rather that interpretation and engagement are active acts of meaning-making. In the Japanese contents industry in particular, and increasingly in other globally prominent contents industries as well, fan and audience engagement and production—the very transnational fandoms that are the subject of this issue—influence and drive official media production both directly and indirectly.

At the same time, however, Iwabuchi's arguments about the inculcation of "cultural odorlessness" in media for export hold up well when applied to previous generations of Japanese media fandom abroad. Accordingly, this volume begins with my own essay, where I explore the origins of anime fandom in the United States from 1975–95 through the archives of anime, science fiction, and furry fandom figure Fred Patten, who played a key role in popularizing anime in the fandom scene in this time period. Patten's generation of fans was introduced to anime through localized adaptations of anime such as *Astro Boy* and *Speed Racer* and, for them, the knowledge that anime was in fact Japanese in origin usually came as something of an epiphany, or a shock. The strategies that anime fans in this time period developed to deal with anime's Japaneseness, once discovered, utilized analog fan networks that arose before the internet and recalled earlier instances of media transmission across national and language boundaries, such as film in Japan during the empire. The empire's aftermath also laid down some of the transmission circuits that early anime fans availed themselves of in order to obtain fresh anime direct from the source.

One criticism of fan studies that has been leveled at online media fandom as well is its neglect of race, racism, and nonwhite fans, all of which have been consistently ignored despite their presence in fandom from the beginning. This issue of *Second Arc* cannot replace Rukmini Pande's timely *Squee from the Margins: Fandom and Race*, but it does go beyond the traditional focus on fans in either Anglophone countries (which usually means the United States) or Japan.[3] Moving across the Atlantic, Salomón Doncel-Moriano Urbano's essay examines the pivotal decade of the 1990s in an entirely different fan culture, namely Spain. While many of the phenomena that Doncel-Moriano discusses—fanzines, fan groups, and conventions—will be familiar in broad outlines to people who participate in fandom around the world, the local particularities of the Spanish Japanese media fan scene emerge as salient and distinct, starting with the embrace of the word "otaku," a term that has a tortuous history in Japan. Doncel-Moriano ultimately concludes that Spanish anime fans were anything but passive consumers: reading through the voluminous archive of fan literature from the 1990s, he finds that fans in that era were active participants in both constructing the Spanish anime and manga industry and instructing society at large about the value of anime and manga as more than "just" children's entertainment. Moreover, the close relationship between fandom and the professional anime and manga industry helped expand the scope for the reception of Japanese media in Spain overall.

Fansubbing and its cousin scanlation were fundamental to fandom before the rise of streaming video services such as Crunchyroll, and initiatives such as Viz Media's digital *Shonen Jump* platform, cut most of the groups practicing them in the English-language fan sphere off at the knees. But these unauthorized practices remain central to fans worldwide who cannot access authorized alternatives, whether for reasons of intellectual property and licensing rights regimes or because they are not proficient in the language(s) in which they are offered. Krystal Urbano's essay explores the phenomenon of fansubbing in Brazil, where anime fans active in the dominant language of Portuguese have not been well-served by linear TV or streaming services. The politics of fansub groups were notorious, if somewhat opaque, before their general demise in Anglophone fandom, and some of those same pluralistic and conflict-driven dynamics are evident in Urbano's analysis, particularly when she explores the ethical reevaluation spurred among fansubbers by the appearance of speed fansub groups. At the same time, Urbano argues that fansubbing has not only become the core distribution method for anime fandom in Brazil but also has created circuits of media distribution that are driving the introduction and spread of East Asian media beyond anime through this space, such as K-dramas. In her fidelity to the common fansubbing experience of conflict and dissent, Urbano calls for a new recognition in fan studies of disagreement and negative emotions generally as drivers of fandom activity itself, and an endemic part of fan interaction rather than a deviation from some idealized community harmony.

Many academics in Japan studies are still prone to talking about "Cool Japan," the belated bureaucratic counterpart to the mukokuseki strategy, as a current rather than past promotional initiative. In reality, both have faded in the past decade, especially after the return of the Abe government saw a new bureaucratic embrace of nationalism in the wake of the 3/11 disasters.

But the mukokuseki argument that Iwabuchi advances can still be a useful analytical tool, as Tomás Grau demonstrates in his essay comparing the global reception of notable video games from *Katamari Damacy* to the *Metal Gear Solid* franchise. The flip side of the fan recognition of Japanese origin is Orientalism, whether techno- or otherwise, and the binary paradigm of Japan/the West still haunts the discourse of Japanese exceptionalism in the video game industry, which Grau highlights, by which Japan is always either "Cool" or "Weird." If fan studies is to adequately recognize media fandom as a postcolonial cyberspace, as Pande argues it is, it must do so by ingesting the theories about Orientalism, techno-orientalism, cultural flows, mediascapes, and domination among which Iwabuchi positioned himself. Video game studies, an even younger field than fan studies, has the opportunity to get ahead of the game by taking aboard these and other theories and discourses from the beginning. In doing so himself, Grau highlights the ways in which ludic categories seeking to sort gameplay aspects into various recognized paradigms interact with assumptions about what is "conventional" versus "unconventional," normalizing a certain kind of game as "typical" in the discourse about video games and potentially constructing vast swathes of games and players as "atypical" or "Other."

Had we so desired, we could have filled this entire issue with essays discussing various aspects of the global smash hit anime *Yuri!!! on Ice* (*YOI*) and its blockbuster fandom. Kristine Santos kicks off the *YOI*-related discussions with her article about fan activities in the Philippines, analyzing the ways in which fans in that country have used recent anime and other fandoms, including *YOI*, to reorient their position in fandom globally through the material production of fanworks. Specifically, Santos argues that Filipino fans are disrupting existing patterns of transcultural flows by producing fan merchandise that has proven popular worldwide, including with traditional Japanese dôjin (fanworks) vendors and through less established digital means of distribution including Tumblr and a new generation of small-producer storefront sites. Santos finds that Filipino fans' fanwork production is also pushing back against the homogenizing tendency of social media platforms and algorithm-driven engagement by highlighting and taking pride in their local and particular national origins, especially through the production of fan goods celebrating the Philippines itself as a site of fandom. Moreover, Santos notes that the rise of Boys' Love (BL) and other fan conventions in the Philippines and in Southeast Asia generally, despite the general lack of stable, licensed methods of media circulation, affords fans another way to disrupt established transcultural flows and centers of transcultural fandom distribution. By making their own zines, stickers, keychains, and more, fans in this region are creating actually existing alternatives to spotty, expensive merchandise import regimes.

Boys' Love fandom has traveled far and wide beyond Japan, particularly throughout other parts of Asia, in the decades since its invention in the 1970s. Through online platforms, it is now possible for fans to participate in both BL and slash or m/m (as it is now being called among younger Angophone fans) fan cultures according to taste and language capability. It would be quite interesting to apply Iwabuchi's ideas about cultural odorlessness and transmission to the genre, which has often been criticized for inattention to the lived realities of actual gay men and gay relationships, particularly in earlier decades. Nice Huang looks at the production and distribution of BL *dôjinshi* (fanzines or fan comics) in Indonesia, where predominant, conservative social mores and harsh laws regarding pornography and queer sexuality might have led to the assumption that such dôjinshi would not find much of a readership. Interviewing four female Indonesian BL dôjinshi creators, Huang instead finds that all four have been able to successfully navigate through the legal gray areas surrounding homoerotic content and the ability to print and distribute it both in Indonesia and in Japan through dôjin vendors such as Toranoana. Online networks and illicit distribution of fanzines have enabled all of these creators both to distribute their own work beyond Indonesia and to remain connected to the larger BL sphere, despite Indonesia's blocking websites such as Tumblr on the grounds that they contain pornographic materials. (In light of Tumblr's December 2018 decision to ban all "adult content," Indonesia officially reversed its previous ban on the site.[4]) The tradeoff, however, is that all of these creators have become somewhat wary of their activities being exposed (at least one of them does not mention her nationality online at all). Based on Huang's interviews, it is evident that Indonesian BL creators have generally adopted a policy of self-censorship in the depiction of explicit sexual scenes (or rather the lack thereof) to mitigate potential consequences should their work be subjected to official scrutiny. Even as Indonesian BL fans and creators continue to successfully fly under the radar, Huang argues that this expanding sphere's subversive potential remains unchecked.

The issue ends, in a sense, where it began, with Lori Morimoto's analysis of *Yuri!!! on Ice* fandom as a contested "contact zone," where previously parallel fans and fan cultures brush up against each other in a welter of languages, norms, and assumptions drawn together by a shared love for an atypical sports anime about elite men's figure skaters. Like most fandoms today, *YOI* fandom is a primarily mediated space that takes place across platforms, languages, and national boundaries, uniting people around the world through social media and in-person events ranging from anime conventions to dôjin events to cafés and pilgrimages. As with most anime fandoms, particularly those that are "simulcast" on Crunchyroll to many countries outside Japan, it was transnational from the beginning, but *YOI*'s unusual, if not unique, appeal for many fans outside the core anime demographics meant that many fans less familiar with the norms of anime and anime fan cultures were drawn into the discussions surrounding the anime and the love story it portrays in multiple languages. Morimoto analyzes these discussions across Twitter, Tumblr, and other platforms, arguing that these platforms and the participation of the show's creators and fans on them proved a remarkable study of "the transcultural implications of real-time global anime distribution and reception," showcasing the multiple and varied subjectivities that different groups of fans with different fandom literacies and different language competencies brought to the show's reception as it aired, actively shaping the discourse about the show as it went on in conversation with the show's creative staff. Many of these fans, Morimoto argues, do not fit easily into the binary, "either/or" categorizations of fans along whatever axes fandom scholars have promoted; instead, the show's reception among different fans showcases the ways in which seemingly monolithic groups are in fact composed of individuals with different, "both/and" plural identities. For Morimoto, transcultural fandom is much more effectively conceptualized as a contact zone rather than as a community. She concludes with a pointed call to Japan studies and its practitioners to do better at recognizing that the matter of "Japan studies" has long since expanded beyond the cul-de-sac of the nation-state, and that to remain relevant and survive in this era, Japan studies must engage with new fields and their knowledge from a genuine standpoint of mutual respect and willingness to learn.

By way of closing, I would like to pay tribute once again to Fred Patten, who passed away at the age of seventy-seven in November 2018, as this issue was in the final stages of preparation. Although Patten will be missed, his legacy lives on, as in 2008 he donated the entire archive of his fandom history to the Eaton Collection of Science Fiction and Fantasy at the University of California, Riverside. The Patten materials are open to researchers, and they represent a vast and invaluable trove recording fandom history in the United States from the bottom up rather than the top down. As I wrote these words in December 2018, Tumblr was on the eve of banning so-called adult content, and had already blocked archival access for researchers and archivists seeking to preserve snapshots of this material, erasing vast swathes of queer and fan history online in the craven pursuit of vanishing, if not fictitious, ad dollars. (Tumblr lost an estimated 30 percent of its traffic in the wake of the porn ban, and in August 2019 Verizon reportedly sold the site for less than $3 million USD, after Yahoo paid $1.1 billion to acquire it in 2013.[5] One user calculated that as of that month each unique user had personally cost the company $2.89.[6]) In this age of the internet, archiving fan materials in both physical and digital form is increasingly important to the preservation and promulgation of fandom history. The fact that archiving is increasingly contested by platform companies makes it even clearer that Patten's example is one fans should consider following in order to keep fandom history alive, just as researchers have a duty to engage with these materials and the fans who created them in order to accurately portray fandom's history and present across boundaries of nation, language, and gender. This issue is one attempt to do exactly that.

Andrea Horbinski
Guest Editor

Notes

1. Henry Jenkins, *Convergence Culture: Where Old and New Media Collide* (New York: New York University Press, 2006).
2. Koichi Iwabuchi, *Recentering Globalization: Popular Culture and Japanese Transnationalism* (Durham: Duke University Press, 2002).
3. Rukmini Pande, *Squee from the Margins: Fandom and Race* (Iowa City: University of Iowa Press, 2018).
4. Jon Russell, "Indonesia Unblocks Tumblr Following Its Ban on Adult Content," *TechCrunch*, December 27, 2018, https://techcrunch.com/2018/12/27/indonesia -unblocks-tumblr/.
5. Shannon Liao, "After the Porn ban, Tumblr Users Have Ditched the Platform as Promised," *The Verge*, March 14, 2019, https://www.theverge.com/2019/3/14 /18266013/tumblr-porn-ban-lost-users-down-traffic; Julia Alexander, "Verizon Is Selling Tumblr to WordPress' Owner," *The Verge*, August 12, 2019, https:// www.theverge.com/2019/8/12/20802639/tumblr-verizon-sold-wordpress -blogging-yahoo-adult-content.
6. tropicalhomestead, "Animetime: God I Love. . . ." Tumblr, August 13, 2019, https://tropicalhomestead.tumblr.com/post/186991465999/animetitle-god-i -love-being-part-of-the.

Transnational Fandom

What You Watch Is What You Are?

Early Anime and Manga Fandom in the United States

ANDREA HORBINSKI

The early years of anime and manga fandom in the United States were an era in which a fascinating welter of developments occurred simultaneously among fans of "geeky" popular culture, particularly science fiction, comics, and gaming, and set the stage for the current structures of fandom as they exist today. Over the course of approximately twenty years in the 1970s and 1980s, American fans attracted to "Japanimation" came to identify themselves as anime fans, a process that was by no means guaranteed to end with that result. Indeed, in their first few decades in the United States both anime and manga went through processes of familiarization, estrangement, and re-adoption that mirrored the experience of other new media in other times and places, particularly that of movies in Japan in the 1900s through 1920s. The evolution of American fans' attitudes toward these media was closely related to the fates of the first companies' attempts to operate for profit in these spaces, and the failures of these companies' efforts to import anime and manga as cartoons and comics essentially conditioned the current regime among both companies and fans that celebrates anime and manga as distinctly Japanese media.

Sociologist Casey Brienza contends that the history of manga publication in the United States before the start of the period she covers in *Manga in America* is more or less irrelevant because "manga was simply not, in short, something that was ever going to work in the comics publishing field" and therefore is not worth discussing at length.[1] While these conclusions are certainly correct for Brienza's study of the American manga industry since 1997, as a historian I cannot agree that those prior decades ought to be disregarded. Failure structures later developments no less than success, and the failures of anime and manga tell a story that is worth adding to the larger narrative of popular culture and its audiences in these decades. Moreover, taking a bottom-up rather than top-down vantage point on this era tells a very different story than the one we can derive from corporate sources; fan cultures are driven by motives other than pure profit, and the archives of fan cultures reveal that even in the years when Japanese media were not selling well, fans were still engaging with them in ways that were consequential. In other words, telling the story of popular culture without engaging with the audiences who consume it creates a fundamentally one-sided and inaccurate narrative.

First, We Take California: Anime Arrives

Early anime fans were drawn to anime not because it was Japanese but because it was an additional form of science fiction or cartoons, in which they had a prior interest. In this respect, the experience of Fred Patten (1940–2018), who had grown up watching cartoons on television and who eventually became a notable figure in science fiction, anime and manga, and furry fandoms, was more or less representative. Living in southern California his entire life, Fred became one of the founders in 1977 of what was christened the "Cartoon/Fantasy Organization" (C/FO), which is now regarded as America's first anime club, eventually serving as its secretary after the organization expanded nationally.[2] The archives of the Fred Patten Collection in the Eaton Library of Science Fiction at the University of California, Riverside, on which this paper principally draws, are full of proof and final copies of Fred's desktop publishing efforts in service of the C/FO and other associated fan events, including science fiction and anime conventions, over the course of more than forty years.

Patten was himself a furry, which may explain the choice of "Sandy," an anthropomorphized female otter-type creature with antennae who served as the group's mascot despite the fact that she had no clear analog in the anime that was one of the group's mainstays. Although Patten later emphasized the C/FO as an anime club, materials in the archives make clear that not every C/FO member nationwide shared this evaluation: Patten himself complained in a report on a trip to Japan in 1986 that the anime goods shops he and his group visited did not contain a lot of "cute animal" merchandise—"cute animals" being the code for characters that drew furry attention used through most of the Patten materials. While cat and bunny girls are certainly not unknown in anime and manga and video games, they were perhaps somewhat less common in the 1980s than they have become in the age of Final Fantasy and the JRPG. In any case, there is quite a difference between the style of animalization of the human form epitomized by Fran from *Final Fantasy XII*

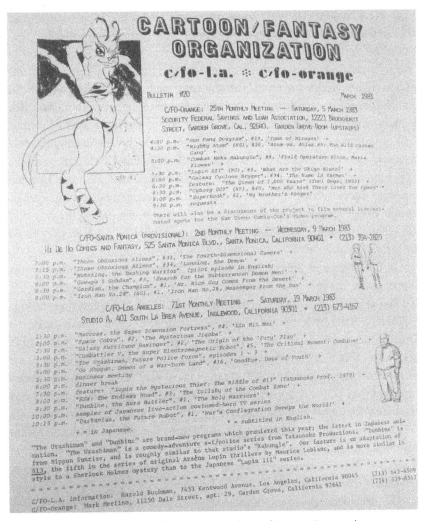

Figure 1. 1983 C/FO newsletter for the Los Angeles and Orange County chapters showing Sandy on the masthead.

and, say, Minnie Mouse or Lola Bunny, who epitomized the American style of anthropomorphization of the animal form that future furries tended to encounter in cartoon consumption from childhood onward in the United States.

The C/FO started in Los Angeles and spread from there to Orange County and the Inland Empire and eventually to other states. Chapters met in a variety of rental spaces, including nerd-related bookstores or game shops, and watched programs of cartoons for several hours on a regular, usually monthly, basis. New chapters in other areas were usually started by people who had attended a few meetings of an established chapter and were inspired to replicate the experience closer to home. Chapter members paid membership fees to cover costs, and chapters themselves paid an annual fee to the C/FO parent organization, run out of Patten's apartment, to maintain their official status. Screening attendees were usually asked to contribute an admission fee at each meeting to cover costs related to the use of the space or the distribution of the programs for the meeting's content, which were usually the sole means of knowing anything about what was being shown in this pre-internet age. Nonmembers paid a surcharge for newsletters and programs in some chapters, incentivizing them to become full-fledged members. In the case of anime, the programs reveal some fascinating commonalities in the way that fans took it upon themselves to wrestle this content into a format they could understand and enjoy.

In the 1970s and 1980s anime was mostly available in the United States in two ways. The first, much less common, way was as a dubbed and adapted version of the show that was broadcast in English on U.S. television stations and that frequently bore little if any relation to the original. (Ironically, the English-language adaptation of *Tetsuwan Atomu* [1963–66, *Astro Boy*], which set the paradigm for this first age of anime adaptations, may have been one of the most faithful of them all.) As the 1980s went on, C/FO members also reported that anime was broadcast with subtitles in some markets; this was the case with *Galaxy Express 999* (1978–81, *Ginga tetsudô 999*) in the New York City area, for example. Second, and much more regularly, however, fans were watching pirated copies of anime that had been recorded from televisions directly onto VHS, usually by people who had access to Japanese-language television channels, primarily in California and Hawai'i, or by members of the U.S. armed forces or their families who were stationed in Japan. A thriving trade in copies of these VHS tapes, sustained by informal networks among fans and occasionally being sold for profit at game or comics shops and conventions, meant that quality was highly variable (since VHS tape, being physical and magnetic, degrades with each copy made) and that it was sometimes difficult to secure sequential runs of episodes of the same shows.

The central problem of early anime fandom was that very few people spoke Japanese. With shows that were dubbed and officially distributed in English vastly outnumbered by those that were not (and in an environment in which local TV stations dropped shows with low ratings mercilessly, frequently leaving devoted viewers with no officially licensed alternatives to see

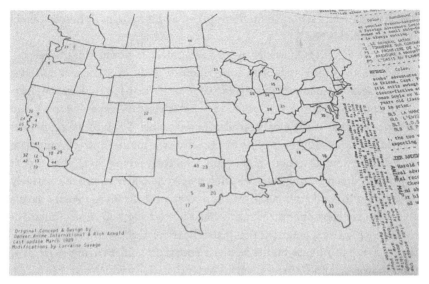

Figure 2. March 1989 map prepared for the C/FO newsletter depicting known anime clubs across the United States and Canada.

the rest of a cancelled series), early anime fans in the United States evolved a number of strategies to mitigate the difficulties of the language barrier. As attested in the Patten archive, these strategies took four principal forms: episode synopses, episode transcripts, Japanese vocabulary building, and live summary and/or translation of shows.

Of these, the first two forms were by far the most common, judging by the preponderance of surviving documents related to them in the Patten archives. Episode synopses were generally written by diligent fans with insider knowledge, whether this took the form of Japanese language skills or access to officially available promotional materials, which Fred Patten, for example, often obtained through his role as a freelance writer/promoter for Japanese animation studios and their shows in the California market and nationally.[3] These synopses were then typed up and photocopied for distribution, either through newsletter mailing networks or their sale at anime screenings. Someone could purchase a set of synopses in order to watch a whole show and know what was going on, or to fill in the gaps in their knowledge of the show if they had not managed to obtain all of the episodes. The fees charged for these synopses were deliberately nominal, usually just enough to recoup printing and shipping costs (if applicable); the belief that being "noncommercial" is a legitimate defense against potential copyright infringement claims was already strong in fandom spaces, and it remains so in some areas of fandom to this day.[4]

Episode synopses, however, were deliberately somewhat high-level, designed to convey the events of an entire show of 26, 39, or 52 or more episodes in a manageable amount of paper and text. Episode transcripts were the strategy of choice for those who wanted to know what was happening in a given episode of anime on the most granular level possible. Given the level of effort involved in translating every line in a twenty-two-minute episode, complete with descriptions of actions and events, and then typing up all that text, it is perhaps unsurprising that full-blown episode transcripts are relatively uncommon in the Patten archive. Those that were archived usually have a price of $1 per copy, one episode each. More interesting, almost all of them include pages with explanations that insist the transcript is an "interpretation," which does not infringe on the Japanese copyright holders in any way; all of them, however, appear to be unvarnished translations, which does constitute copyright infringement under U.S. law.

The fannish attitude toward the rights holders and the companies involved in officially licensing and distributing anime in the United States at the time was an outgrowth of the deferential posture evidenced in these notes—notwithstanding the fact that most of the anime fans consumed was pirated in one way or another. American anime fans generally saw themselves as boosters of anime in their local broadcast markets, and they aspired to official acknowledgment of their activities in their roles as early adopters, which they actually achieved to some degree in the late 1970s. As Fred Patten related in a 2001 book chapter, years of contact between the C/FO in Southern California and Japanese anime studios began with a visit from Tezuka himself to a C/FO meeting in 1978. This meeting culminated in "a tour group of about thirty Japanese cartoonists and animators," including Tezuka, who attended the San Diego Comic Con (SDCC) in 1980, "so they could see for themselves what an audience Japanese animation was developing in the United States." Although nothing much came of this tour at the institutional level, according to Patten, "the influence on the fledgling anime fans of having met some of the most popular Japanese cartoonists, and the concept that fans were performing an important cultural service by helping to introduce Japanese animation to Americans, had a significant effect for years."[5]

But the influence in this era was not all one way. In a fine irony, the visit of (future) Japanese anime industry figures to American fandom in 1980 that was to have a lasting impact on Japanese fan cultures as a whole was not that of Tezuka and company to SDCC. Rather, it was that of Okada Toshio (b. 1958) and Takeda Yasuhiro (b. 1957) to the science fiction convention Worldcon in Boston (specifically, Noreascon Two), which directly inspired their bid to host the now-legendary DaiCon III convention in Osaka in 1981 and launched them on the path to founding General Products and Gainax. Unheralded, unanticipated, and unknown as Okada and Takeda were (the exact opposite of the deference shown to Tezuka and his colleagues in San Diego), their Worldcon experience ultimately changed fandom worldwide in another example of the transnational influence of fannish border-crossing.[6]

Languages and Letters: Speaking for Anime

The deference shown toward rights-holders in the fannish newsletters was the flip side of an argument that would eventually bring down the C/FO as a national organization and reconfigure the U.S. anime fandom scene by the beginning of the 1990s, namely, the ongoing argument about pirated versus officially distributed media and what moral obligation fans had to media companies, if any. The arguments about piracy were and are partly a consequence of an exaggerated idea of the importance of what was a small minority of early adopters to the commercial potential of officially licensed media.[7] In the 1970s and 1980s, however, this attitude most often manifested in campaigns to either reverse a cancellation decision or to get a local TV station to put anime on the air.

Letter-writing campaigns had been pioneered in the science fiction fandom community in the late 1960s, when Bjo Trimble (b. 1933), assisted by her husband John, spearheaded the grassroots letter-writing campaign that successfully resulted in the production of the third season of *Star Trek* (1966–69), reversing CBS's decision to cancel the series after just two seasons. Judging by the contents of the Patten archive, anime campaigns had a mixed record. For example, the June 1982 bulletin of the C/FO–New York chapter informs fans of the impending cancellation of the *Galaxy Express 999* anime in that market:

> As some of you know, Entel Communications has now started its programming at 10:00pm Sundays, instead of 9:00pm. C/FOer Patricia Malone has discovered that *Galaxy Express 999* will go off the air this week and there is no planned replacement animation. The people at

Entel feel that "not many 'children' are up at 10:00pm Sunday evening," hence no sponsors.

Naomi Saraki, the person who does the subtitles, believes that if she can get enough *letters* from people to show the higher-ups there is an audience, perhaps something could be done. We've asked this once before; if everyone would please write to Entel, perhaps we could get them to reinstate animation in their programming.

As it happens, this particular C/FO–New York campaign was a success. The August 1982 bulletin contained an update, informing fans: "In September, Mater & Tetsuro will be back from vacation to continue their trips on the *Galaxy Express 999*. Many thanks to everyone who wrote in and helped to get *GE 999* back on the air. The people at ENTEL now know that their animation appeals to more than just kids." Six months later, in the newsletter for the 32nd monthly screening, the C/FO–New York was at it again, asking members to write to the local station WQR-TV9 on behalf of Fuji Television, which was "planning to introduce Reiji [sic] (Captain Harlock, *Galaxy Express 999*) Matsumoto's animated series, 'Queen of a Thousand Years,' to american [sic] audiences. It is being translated into English and because it is not a violence-oriented series, it will survive the transition nearly intact." The C/FO–New York cast this campaign in terms of mutual self-interest, saying that "Fuji will need support from the US fans to get this series on television. . . . Only letters will work; *lots* of letters. They need proof that there is an audience for the program. So, if you want some serious & intelligent animation on network TV, write."

Letter-writing campaigns were by no means guaranteed to be successful, and a flyer entitled "Star Blazers in New York" from around the same time as these C/FO–New York bulletins provides some hints as to why that could be. After outlining the current outlook in New York City for the broadcast of *Star Blazers* (1979–84), the now-infamous English-language adaptation of three sliced and diced *Space Battleship Yamato* shows (1974, 1978, 1989, *Uchū senkan Yamato*), the flyer detailed seven guidelines for fan letter writers, including not to call the TV station directly, not to write form letters, to mention their age and request a later time slot for the show, to be polite ("Rude letters get us no place, and will hinder more than help"), to "mention that you have friends who have also seen the show and enjoyed it. But try not to mention that you are part of a letter writing campaign that is organized," not to write cut-and-

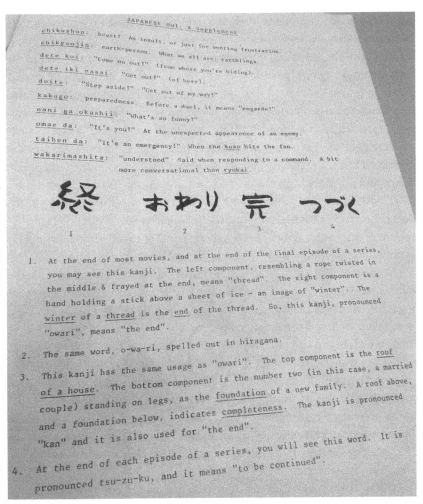

Figure 3. "Japanese 001," translated by Eddie Wood, circulated by the C/FO–New York in its December 1983 newsletter.

paste type letters on the grounds that "this will set us back, and will give the impression that we are just a bunch of little kids," and not to "get over involved with one letter. Your letter should be short and to the point." At the end of the flyer, there is an address to which fans could send a self-addressed stamped envelope if they wanted to join the local *Star Blazers* fan club.

The third strategy available to anime fans was studying Japanese, which, judging from the newsletters, usually took the form of guides to catchphrases and/or common expressions likely to recur in a given series or across anime in general. This strategy also seems to have been relatively uncommon; it was not until the 1990s and 2000s that college-level Japanese teachers in the United States began reporting that anime and manga were driving enrollments in Japanese-language classes. One example of such a guide contains brush-painted reproductions of kanji and hiragana phrases used in television, specifically those for "the end" and "to be continued," as well as explanations of the radicals in the kanji themselves. Another vocabulary list circulated by the C/FO–New York in December 1983, including such common words and phrases as "gambatte" (defined literally as "Try hard!" or "Go for it!"), "hoshi" (usually "star," sometimes "planet"), was defined in terms of the *Galaxy Express 999* anime. Its definition of "Isoide" reads: "'Hurry!' 999 is pulling out of the station, Maytel & Tetsuro are running to catch it, the Conductor leans out the window, 'Isoide! Hayaku!'"

The fourth strategy of which anime fans availed themselves was by far the most interesting, namely that of live summary/translation at anime screenings. For whatever reason, this strategy, called "narration" in the newsletters, seems to have been practiced principally by the fans of the C/FO–New York, which began in 1980.[8] In "narration," bilingual fans, usually women, would live translate/interpret the anime for the benefit of their fellow non-Japanese-speaking fans. The undated newsletter that announced the 53rd monthly screening of the C/FO–New York chapter, for example, states that at the previous screening (presumably January 1985, given the reference to Disney's *The Black Cauldron* [1985] as "upcoming") chapter president Patricia "Pat" Malone "narrated the *Macross* episode, #36, which was given a wealth of applause when it ended."

Other C/FO–New York newsletters, however, betray the enormous amount of effort that these fan volunteers put into the screenings and the tensions that arose. In a letter published in the July 1983 bulletin and dated June 20 of that year, Pat Malone registered her discontent with her fellow fans along several axes, opening with the question, "How come people always ask for something in English but as soon as it's shown some people are grumbling about it and, as what happened last meeting, have it pulled for some Japanese cartoons." Malone's question was apparently prompted by a failed attempt to screen the animated feature *Winds of Change* (1979, *Hoshi no Orufeusu*) the previous month; after twenty minutes, popular demand at the screening led to turning off the movie and switching to anime. "We are the CARTOON FANTASY ORGANIZATION not the Japanese Cartoon Fan Association," Malone wrote. "We are not exclusively Japanese cartoons many of us want to see something else, something different. Some people have gotten to be like the censorship we all complain about, only it's 'if it isn't Japanese, it's no good.'"

Malone had put a significant amount of personal labor into the club, as she reminded people: "I have worked hard to get the club a meeting place, to get various and new programs. Also to get translations of programs. (I gave a narration of the first 2 episodes of 'SSX.') As much as I love Harlock, I don't want a steady diet of him. I sometimes want to see something different, something in English like others in the club I know of. But if the ones who just want to watch giant robots and space battles get their way, the club will loose [sic] members and dwindle to nothing." Interestingly enough, given the contents of her letter, Malone signed off with the Japanese phrase "Dewa shitsurei itashi-masita," which literally means "I have disturbed you," but in context could mean anything from "Excuse me" to a much ruder phrase. In the next bulletin, Malone informed members that the C/FO–New York newsletter writer job, and by implication the presidency of the chapter, had fallen to her by dint of no one else volunteering. Her report from the August screening was that "the change of control was announced and accepted by the members."

That same August 1983 screening featured a rare instance of a male Japanese speaker assisting with narration, this time one Hiroto Mandai, who helped Malone with an episode of SSX and one Jim Kapostzas with "the narration of the feature, YAMATO: THE CONCLUDING CHAPTER. Hiroto was given a hearty thank you and a round of applause for his help." Mandai maintained a correspondence with Malone after he returned to Japan, writing to her in October 1983 about the state of anime and manga in Japan, mentioning Adachi Mitsuru and Takahashi Rumiko by name (and in American rather than Japanese name order); Malone published his letter verbatim in the December 1983 bulletin. It seems that "narration" sometimes consisted of reading the English subtitles aloud to the audience, which Kapostzas and two attendees, "the Moriarty brothers," are stated to have done at other times, as did Malone herself, as at the 41st meeting in 1984, when she "with the help of the people in the front row read the subtitles to MY YOUTH IN ARCADIA." In the same bulletin, Malone informed members of the start of a campaign trying to keep the animated show *Inspector Gadget* (1983–86) on the air, and that "Urusai Yatsura means Those Annoying Aliens or Those Noisy Aliens."

The fact that the C/FO screening attendees protested *Winds of Change* is significant given the film's tortured bi-national origins: released by Sanrio as the rock generation's answer to *Funtasia* (1940), it consisted of five short retellings of segments from Ovid's *Metamorphoses* and was directed and written by a Japanese animator, Takashi, but was nonetheless created entirely in Hollywood. The movie performed dismally upon its initial U.S. release in 1979 under the English title *Metamorphoses*; after trimming seven minutes, the studio rereleased it under the title *Winds of Change*, which was the version that went over so poorly at the New York screening.[9] Although certainly not "anime" in the sense of limited animation that was made for television in Japan, the argument could certainly be made that *Winds of Change* was nonetheless "Japanese animation," or "Japanimation" as it was called then. Were the C/FO members reacting solely to the movie's language, as Malone claimed? Or was it just that *Winds of Change* was a bad movie, as the box office returns indicated?

The practice of "narration" in the C/FO–New York in the early 1980s recalls nothing so much as the prewar institution in Japanese film known as the *benshi* (narrators of films who interpreted movies live for audiences in the theater). Like anime fans in the United States, Japanese movie audiences faced a language barrier when watching films made abroad even in the silent era, as they could not read the intertitles in other languages. Japanese film promoters hit upon the notion of the benshi, often going so far as to invent their own sound effects. (Before the advent of talkies, movie scores in the United States were most often provided by in-house accompanists who improvised, usually on piano.) Benshi were so popular, and so institutionalized as part of what made movies movies, that they continued well into the talkie era despite multiple attempts by promoters of so-called Pure Film and the fascist Japanese state to stamp them out through various means, as detailed by film historian Aaron Gerow in *Visions of Japanese Modernity*.[10]

The key point of comparison, highlighted by the similarities between benshi and fan narration, is how movies were treated in Japan in the early twentieth century and how Japanese animation was treated in the United States after 1963. Gerow's book is in part an argument for recognizing that early Japanese cinema was always a transnational phenomenon and a transnational negotiation, contrary to a discourse of film in Japan that has, in his words, relied upon "asserting a clear border between Japan and the West when narrating a history of cinema rife with border crossings."[11] The same dichotomy has been applied to anime, and it does not hold up any better: how should a transnationally produced animated feature like *Wings of Change* be categorized? (And who should get the blame for its failures?) Does the outsourcing of the animation for *The Last Unicorn* (1982) by Rankin and Bass to the Japanese studio Topcraft (which later became the core of Studio Ghibli) make that movie "anime" or "Japanese animation?" What about anime in which the bulk of the animation labor was outsourced to Korea or Taiwan or Vietnam? What about American cartoons from the 1970s whose animation was done in Japan, in whole or in part?

Epiphanies and Spectacles: Crossing Boundaries of Genre and Nation

The central experience of early anime fans in the United States was often the revelation—frequently narrated in terms of having an epiphany—that many of the cartoons that they had enjoyed in earlier years had been made in Japan. Patten himself made this connection in 1970 thanks to an encounter with the manga version of *The Man from U.N.C.L.E.* at Westercon, a West Coast science fiction convention, which led to his realization that *Astro Boy*'s origins lay across the Pacific.[12] These epiphanies were powered by the fact that before anime was "Japanimation" it was just cartoons; *Astro Boy, Speed Racer* (1967–68, *Mahha GôGôGô*), and other shows were dubbed into English and shown on TV in the States with no remark on their national origins or being "strange." As Patten summarized, "To Americans, these half-hour TV cartoons were indistinguishable from most American TV animation. . . . So the cartoons from Japan were not thought of by the public as 'Japanese animation.' If their origins were realized at all, they were considered to be just part of a vague 'foreign animation' category."[13] In Patten's telling, when comics and science fiction fans discovered Japanese anime as such, beginning in 1976 with mecha shows, "there was considerable culture shock."[14]

Aaron Gerow writes of cinema in Japan that "Certainly cinema . . . was seen as alien only after it was treated as familiar (as a *misemono*)."[15] When cinema was introduced to Japan, in other words, it was treated not as inherently foreign, Western, or modern, but simply as another form of spectacle, an entertaining thing to watch (*misemono*). Just as the earliest films in the United States and Europe were shown as part of the programs at vaudeville shows or (via kinetoscopes and the like) as one of multiple attractions in amusement arcades, like those on Coney Island, film in Japan before the 1910s was not marked out as special or separate but was naturalized as merely another kind of entertaining performance. So too were Japanese animated TV shows first treated the same as other, American-produced TV animation; it was only after they were "discovered" and popularized as "Japanimation" by Patten and his fellow fans that anime became marked as alien and Other, albeit (just like films in Japan) in a "good," entertaining way. This urge to treat anime as Other was what led Patricia Malone to castigate her fellow New York–C/FOers for their alleged unthinking preference for Japanese-language materials. It was also (among other things) what led to the split between science fiction (SF) and animanga fandoms in the 1990s, which Patten and other older fans lamented: "it used to be that fans who enjoyed Japanese animated SF also enjoyed American SF movies, TV programs, novels, and comic books. They were satisfied with a Japanimation video room as part of a comprehensive general SF convention," Patten wrote in 1994, "Most of them still are, but now some fans are organizing separate 'anime and manga' conventions to concentrate on this Japanese visual SF alone."[16]

Even Patten, who surely ought to have known better, persisted in equating all of anime and manga solely with science fiction. "I can't help feeling that people are missing the real point," he wrote in that same 1994 article, "The point is not that this is Japanese animation, but that it is science fiction animation—or that it is animated SF. This missed point is emphasized every time somebody asks why Japanese animation is becoming so popular in America, the implication being, what is there about the Japanese cultural mystique that is so entrancing, which the animated cartoons of other countries can't match?" Patten's sidebar notes on the article, written a decade later, in 2004, acknowledge that "in 1994, anime's appeal may have been mostly as animated SF and fantasy. That is certainly no longer true."[17]

To be fair to Patten, the equation of anime and manga with science fiction was naturalized by what kinds of anime and manga were exported to the U.S. markets for the first twenty years after the first anime screening in the United States in 1975, and particularly in the 1980s. The experience of manga in the States in that decade makes clear that both anime and manga were being slotted into pre-existing fan spaces and markets; manga's general history in the United States mirrors that of anime, but (in a reversal of the historical relationship between the two in Japan) on a more compressed timeline and very much in anime's wake. In the 1980s, manga was sold alongside comics, which were entering a creative and capitalist cul-de-sac after their retreat from urban newsstands to dedicated comics shops, frequently in suburban strip malls and shopping centers. This retreat to the suburbs and the abandonment of large swaths of comics' former broad audiences in favor of focusing on white male customers was matched by a transformation in mainstream comics content, which, in literature scholar Ramzi Fawaz's analysis, "*devalued* the kinds of gender and sexual transformations that superhero comics like *The X-Men* had celebrated in the mid-1970s."[18] Manga was being treated as

XENON: Return of a Heavy Metal Warrior

by Fred Burke

Xenon, Masaomi Kanzaki's fast-paced heavy metal warrior melodrama, burst noisily onto the U.S. comics scene in late 1987, the year of the American manga explosion. The fourth Viz/Eclipse International title, *Xenon*, quickly overtook *The Legend of Kamui* and *Area 88* to join *Mai, the Psychic Girl* at the top of the biweekly manga hit parade.

With the historical/ninja, military/aviation, and literary/psychic bases covered, it had certainly seemed time to roll out a true superhero soap opera, something the manga readers had been clamoring for all summer.

Xenon fit the bill, giving us one more view of the huge variety of material being published in Japan.

Having edited the translations of Sanpei Shirato's *Kamui* (by Saburo Fuji and Toren Smith) and Kaoru Shintani's *Area 88* (by Fuji and James Hudnall), I was next up at bat as Fuji's co-translator, under the able editorial guidance of Eclipse's Letitia Glozer and Viz's Abra Numata.

I couldn't have asked for a more entertaining assignment.

The powers that be at Viz and Eclipse may have chosen *Xenon* for its hot art, cyborg transformations and rip-roaring action, but thrust into the center of Kanzaki's intensely innocent yet gore-filled world, I immediately fell in love with a cast of characters who live on in my mind like old high school friends: Asuka Kano, the valiant bully-fighter and kitten-saver who would be turned into the amnesiac cyborg Xenon; Sonoko, destined to fall pitifully in love with a man she did not understand; Risa, Sonoko's valley girl/tomboy best friend, afraid of losing her closest compadre; Ryuji, Asuka's ex-rival and a gangleader without a

(continued on the next page)

Figure 4. Cover of *Viz-in*, vol. 2, no. 10, promotional newsletter distributed by VIZ Media, c. 1990, depicting the English release of *Xenon* (1986–87, Jûki kôhe Zenon).

familiar, in other words, in that it was slotted into current American "mainstream" comics culture, which at the time was both masculinized and oriented toward science fiction in a broad sense, ranging from superheroes to SF-ish action tales. Viz and Dark Horse, the two main companies that tried to sell manga as comics, licensed properties that would appeal to established comics fans and marketed them in locations frequented only by those same fans, who were constructed as male and (usually) white by both comics companies and most comics shops. Accordingly, there was no sense that manga could appeal to anyone beyond this presumed core comics demographic, regardless of the existence of female and nonwhite comics fans then and now.

Consequently, SF titles like *Ghost in the Shell, Akira,* and action manga like *Xenon* (1986–87) feature heavily in the promotional materials preserved in the Patten archive from these years. There was no attempt to import titles marketed to people beyond this demographic in Japan (i.e., shôjo, josei, and many seinen titles) because those audiences were presumed to have no U.S. equivalent. As Casey Brienza notes, moreover, the process of making manga familiar—what she calls "domesticating"—was particularly labor-intensive in these years, "involving reversing pages so that they would read in a left-to-right Western-style orientation and retouching artwork to remove and replace Japanese sound effects before manga fans stateside began demanding that companies present manga "unchanged."[19] Only when manga broke out of the comics market with the rise of shojo titles such as *Sailor Moon* (1991–97) in the 1990s did it become "strange" and "Japanese"; it did so, moreover, by attaching itself to trade book publishing. As Brienza summarizes, "While manga was not successful as a comic, and comics were not usually successful as books, by constructing the medium as something distinct from American comics, manga was able to become a book—and some manga series have gone on to sell millions of copies in the trade book market."[20] The treatment of manga not as "Japanese comics" but as an entirely distinct, alien medium enabled manga to rise to unprecedented heights of popularity in the States and worldwide. In turn, the popularity of manga has wrought many changes on the U.S. comics industry—but that's another story.

Conclusion: Coming of Age in Fandom

The early history of anime and manga fandom in the United States demonstrates that the specific history of adoption of anime and manga into existing

Figure 5. "Save Our Sailors" flyer promoting the fan campaign to return *Sailor Moon* to American broadcast.

U.S. fan cultures has many similarities to the adoption of cinema into Japan in the early twentieth century and, for that matter, of comics into Japan in the late nineteenth century. The problems of media adoption across boundaries of nation and language are thus to some extent medium-specific rather than nationally determined, as the parallel evolution of benshi in Japanese movie theaters and narration among U.S. anime fans indicates. Audiences have grappled with these same problems not as a consequence of national or cultural characteristics but due to the more prosaic technical characteristics of these media themselves: in the case of both anime and movies, audiences first dealt with a "new" form of media by naturalizing it as a pre-existing form of media, ignoring or effacing differences of language, culture, and national origin, as well as technical specifications. Cinema in Japan was treated as a form of spectacle; Japanese cartoons were consumed first as cartoons and then as science fiction. Over time, however, these differences became increasingly apparent and their significance became increasingly elevated by audiences, finally reaching the point where these media could no longer be subsumed into pre-existing categories. As a result, SF and anime fandom cultures in the United States have developed on different tracks for the past twenty-five years.

The first twenty years of anime and manga fandom in the United States saw explosive growth in the popularity of these media among a rapidly growing group of fans, from science fiction devotees in the 1970s and 1980s to an increasingly broad and increasingly younger swath of the population in the 1990s. The broadcast of the *Sailor Moon* (1992–97) anime in syndication in the States in 1995 probably marks the end of this "childhood" era, which makes it only fitting that the anime's initial syndication was a failure; it returned to U.S. broadcast only after a successful fan campaign. In the twenty years between Fred Patten and Wendell Washer screening anime for the Los Angeles Science Fiction Society in July 1975 and the debut of *Sailor Moon,* the pre-existing structures of fandom—both in terms of existing fannish audiences and of the companies that sought to monetize the growing enthusiasm for anime and manga—had a huge influence on the development of the U.S. anime and manga industries. Those industries also began to come into their own after 1995, mostly after having shaken off a rocky early history of failed ventures and false starts conditioned by those same pre-existing fandom conditions. In other words, this history mattered in ways both positive and negative to the people who made significant profits in the U.S. anime and manga booms of the late 1990s to mid-2000s.

Taken altogether, the Patten archive and the history of early anime and manga fandom it contains demonstrate that the history of anime and manga in general and in the States specifically has always been one of border crossings, in which media and their industries and audiences on both sides of the Pacific have influenced one another in repeated and frequently surprising ways. This transnational history is not one in which cultures are odorless or borders are nonexistent. But it is one in which border-crossing has repeatedly proved to be possible, meaningful, and mutually consequential.

Andrea Horbinski holds a PhD in modern Japanese history with a designated emphasis in new media from the University of California, Berkeley. She has discussed anime, manga, fandom, and Japanese history at conventions and conferences on five continents, and her articles on manga and fandom in Japan and online have appeared in *Transformative Works and Cultures, Convergence, Internet Histories,* and *Mechademia.* Her book manuscript, "Manga's Global Century," is a history of Japanese comics from 1905–89.

Notes

Previous versions of this paper were given as talks at the 2014 Mechademia conference and at Anime Expo 2016. I would like to thank the audience participants in the Q&A sessions at both venues, as well as the librarians, archivists, and staff of the Eaton Collection at UC Riverside in Riverside, California, upon which this paper is founded. My trip was supported by a summer research grant from the Center for New Media at the University of California, Berkeley. All quotations not otherwise attributed in this article draw from materials held in the Fred Patten Collection at UCR.

1. Casey Brienza, *Manga in America: Transnational Book Publishing and the Domestication of Japanese Comics* (New York: Bloomsbury, 2016), 42.
2. Fred Patten, *Watching Anime, Reading Manga: 25 Years of Essays and Reviews* (Berkeley, Calif.: Stone Bridge Press, 2004), 24–25.
3. Patten, *Watching Anime, Reading Manga,* 9–10.
4. Mikhail Koulikov, "Fighting the Fan Sub War: Conflicts between Media Rights Holders and Unauthorized Creator/distributor Networks" (*Transformative Works and Cultures,* no. 5, doi:10.3983/twc.2010.0115), 4.2–4.3.
5. Patten, *Watching Anime, Reading Manga,* 59.
6. Andrea Horbinski, *Manga's Global Century: A History of Japanese Comics, 1905–1989* (PhD diss., University of California, Berkeley, 2017), 237–39.
7. Koulikov, "Fighting the Fan Sub War," 4.6.
8. Patten, *Watching Anime, Reading Manga,* 28.
9. Jerry Beck, *The Animated Movie Guide* (Chicago: Chicago Reader Press, 2005), 166–67.
10. Aaron Gerow, *Visions of Japanese Modernity: Articulations of Cinema, Nation, and Spectatorship, 1895–1925* (Berkeley: University of California Press, 2010), 40–64.
11. Gerow, *Visions of Japanese Modernity,* 19.
12. Jason Thompson, "Fred Patten and Graphic Story World," *Pulp,* n.d. (ca. 2001); archived at https://web.archive.org/web/20041020025452/www.pulp-mag .com/archives/5.09/interview_patten.shtml (accessed August 18, 2016).
13. Patten, *Watching Anime, Reading Manga,* 54.

14. Patten, 56.

15. Gerow, *Visions of Japanese Modernity*, 64.

16. Patten, *Watching Anime, Reading Manga*, 20.

17. Patten, 20.

18. Ramzi Fawaz, *The New Mutants: Superheroes and the Radical Imagination of American Comics* (New York: New York University Press, 2016), 203, emphasis original.

19. Brienza, *Manga in America*, 42.

20. Brienza, 43.

The Genesis of the Otaku Phenomenon in Spain

A Journey through Fanzines, Associations, and Conventions during the 1990s

SALOMÓN DONCEL-MORIANO URBANO

For the early community of Spanish otaku, manga and anime were "expressions of Japanese art," comparable to painting and literary masterpieces.[1] Their veneration of these genres, their close relation with the industry, and their influence in the construction and development of the current state of affairs surrounding manga and anime in Spain cannot be properly understood without insight into the history of the Spanish otaku community's development throughout the 1990s. The voice of fandom can be heard in manga and anime conventions and read in the nonprofit fanzines they created. The role of otaku associations should not be underestimated either, since they not only contributed to the dissemination of manga and anime but also endeavored to minimize the effects of censorship and bans that these examples of Japanese popular culture faced during their first steps into the Spanish market.

Most research on manga and anime in the Spanish context revolves around such topics as fansubs and scanlations, the present state of affairs of the anime and manga industry, and literary criticism of animated masterpieces and their adaptations into different formats and languages. However, little attention has been paid to the origins of the Spanish fan revolution through the prism of otaku literature from the 1990s, the nature of the Spanish otaku community, and otaku interaction with these cultural products and the industry in that period.

This essay details the rise of Spanish manga and anime fandom in the 1990s, which has been largely overlooked in Anglophone and Japanese-language studies of anime fandom to date. How did the fan revolution originate? When did Spanish otaku start translating manga for their fellow fans? Where did they express their opinions? And, last but not least, how did some otaku manage to start their careers in the manga and anime industry, resulting in the current state of affairs? These are the main questions this essay addresses regarding the otaku phenomenon in the Spanish context. This discussion of Spanish otaku may be useful in shedding light onto other topics currently under discussion in fan studies.

The Term "Otaku"

Spanish fandom started to use the term "otaku" to refer to the community of fans during the late 1990s. The fan literature that this article is based upon uses the word "otaku" repeatedly, proudly alluding to the fan community of manga, anime, and Japanese popular culture of that time. According to the components of some major manga and anime associations from the 1990s, the use of this epithet was derived from the song "Tatakae," the opening theme of *Otaku no Video*, which became the hymn of the first generation of Spanish otaku. Under this premise, and considering Panini's publication of a Spanish magazine about manga, anime, and Japanese culture, *Otaku Bunka*, since 2016, I have found it appropriate to refer to Spanish fandom as "otaku" since it mirrors the perspective and self-conception of fans from the genesis of the phenomenon to the present day.

The Origins of the Fan Revolution

Japanese comics and animated series enjoy a leading, privileged position in Spain and around the world nowadays, due in part to the technological progress of the last decades. However, only two decades ago, the presence of anime and manga on Spanish TV channels and bookstore shelves was infrequent. A brief overview of the first commercialized manga and anime in Spain will help familiarize the reader with the genesis of this transnational phenomenon.

The Advent of Anime Productions

Claiming that one specific anime was the first to be broadcast in Spain could be considered risky and imprecise, although previous research points out that the first Japanese animations translated and dubbed were aired between the late 1970s and early 1980s.[2] That period coincided with the arrival of animated productions such as *Kimba the White Lion* (*Janguru taitei*), *Speed Racer* (*Mach Gogogo*), and *Mazinger Z*, broadcast on TVE, the main national state-owned public-service television broadcaster in Spain (Figure 1). The 1980s brought to Spain popular shôjo series such as *Candy Candy* and *Princess Knight* (*Ribon no kishi*), both of which were aired on TVE on Sunday afternoons.[3] However, it was not until the late 1980s, when three popular anime series would break into the homes of children and teenagers, that the Spanish otaku phenomenon would start to take shape. These three shônen anime were *Dragon Ball*, *Saint Seiya* and *Captain Tsubasa*, aired for the first time on Canal Sur, Telecinco, and TVE, respectively.[4] Other anime series, such as *Sailor Moon* (*Bishôjo senshi Seeraa Mûn*), *Ranma ½*, and *City Hunter* followed, targeting broader and more diverse audiences. The first serialized manga soon supported the dissemination of anime on TV, having a decisive impact within the otaku phenomenon in Spain.

Title	Year of first broadcast in Spain	Original broadcast date
Kimba the White Lion	1969	1965
Speed Racer	1971	1967
Mazinger Z	1978	1972
Candy Candy	1984	1976
Princess Knight	1987	1967
Dragon Ball	1989	1986
Saint Seiya	1990	1986
Captain Tsubasa	1991	1983
Sailor Moon	1993	1992
Ranma ½	1994	1989
City Hunter	1994	1987
Marmalade Boy	1998	1994

Figure 1. Timeline of anime works cited.

The Arrival of Manga in Spain

Tebeosfera, a reputable online portal for comics as well as a reliable source of information about media in the Spanish language, records the first manga extract published in Spain in the double issue 137/138 of the magazine *Cavall Fort* in December 1968: *Tonda Haneko-jô* (*Miss Tonda Haneko*) by Kitazawa Rakuten (Figure 2).[5] This one-page extract, which was curiously translated into Catalan and not into Spanish, was followed by *The Life of Mao Tse Tung* (*Mô Takutô den*), a biographical manga, published by Spanish publishing house *Grijalbo*, that would become the first single-volume manga printed in Spain. Its pages were flipped to follow the reading direction of the Roman alphabet, and it was surprisingly translated directly from Japanese, in contrast to the manga that followed during the 1990s, the vast majority of which were translated from the English-language North American editions.[6] In 1984, *La Cúpula* published *Life is Sad and Other Stories*, a collection of short stories by Tatsumi Yoshihiro, following the same format. The Spanish edition of this compilation included a preface by Spanish philosopher, journalist, and writer Josep María Carandell, who underscored that the translation and dissemination of Japanese comics in the Western world faced several challenges stemming from the particular linguistic and cultural features of Japanese society.[7]

Title	Year of initial release in Spain	Original release date
Miss Tonda Haneko	1968	1928
The Life of Mao Tse Tung	1979	1973
Life is Sad and Other Stories	1984	
Candy Candy	1984	1975
The Fist of the North Star	1992	1983
Crying Freeman	1992	1986
Dragon Ball	1992	1984
Ranma ½	1993	1987
Detective Conan	1998	1994
Marmalade Boy	1998	1992
One Piece	1999	1997

Figure 2. Timeline of manga works cited.

In 1984, *Bruguera* released *Candy Candy*, the first shôjo manga distributed in Spain, written by Mizuki Kyoko and illustrated by Igarashi Yumiko, which narrated the drama of an abandoned orphan girl, taken in by the orphanage Pony's Home around the start of the twentieth century. *Candy Candy*'s animation substantially supported and even promoted its comic version counterpart and, in fact, the manga was published by way of merchandising after the success of the animated series. Some signs of Westernization in *Candy Candy* were the flipping and coloring of pages, and the adaptation to the customary

American comic book "floppy" format resembling magazines. However, it was not until 1992, with the opening of *Planeta deAgostini's* manga line, that *The Fist of the North Star (Hokuto no ken), Crying Freeman,* and *Dragon Ball* would unleash the manga revolution.

The *Dragon Ball* Boom: From Pirated Photocopies to Official Merchandise

The Spanish press soon hailed the unprecedented success of *Dragon Ball* as a "social phenomenon" and as the "culmination of an extraordinary process of popular fascination."[8] *Dragon Ball* became the first manga to be serialized in Spain on a weekly basis, with two simultaneous editions in two different languages: 100,000 monthly copies in Catalan (one of Spain's co-official languages), and 50,000 in Spanish.[9] It released tremendous passion among fans, who soon started to look for the manga counterpart of the animated series they watched on TV. The early and mid-1990s witnessed fans' insatiable desire to read the new adventures of Son Goku, a fact that prompted several fanzines to include photocopies of untranslated Japanese releases of *Dragon Ball.* These extracts featured subjective explanations of what happened in the panels and even with what seem to be the first dated examples of Spanish fan translations of manga.[10]

Likewise, in light of the absence of merchandise between 1990 and 1992, a black market emerged for photocopies from the original manga, along with Japanese-produced sticker albums and photos taken from the anime series.[11] These pirated black and white photocopies were being exchanged among children in schools. Allegedly, some stationery shops in Andalusia and Catalonia joined the black market, also selling unauthorized black and white posters of the series. In December 1991, *Panini* (publisher of comic books, magazines and merchandise) obtained the rights to commercialize a full-color sticker collection with images that had been directly extracted from anime frames. The initial print run of five million envelopes and one hundred thousand albums sold out within a month, overtaking the trade of photocopies.[12] The sticker fever invaded the main street markets in the cities of Barcelona and Madrid where kids and their parents went every weekend to find their "missing stickers,"[13] creating a demand for anime-related products that grew to the point of requiring police intervention.[14] The rapid rise of "sticker fever" highlights the scope of the otaku phenomenon since its inception. Unquestionably, the phenomenon was escaping the hands of the manga and anime industries, which either did not respond to the needs of the emerging otaku community or did so only after a considerable delay. On the contrary, fandom was starting to get used to finding and even (re)creating alternative merchandise which they exchanged with and disseminated to the rest of the otaku community. Phrased another way, fans were claiming faster releases, more merchandise, and a place to purchase and exchange all types of material and ideas related to the manga and anime they consumed.

Manga and Anime Conventions

As evidenced by the enterprising attitude of fans in their attempts to gather unpublished manga and merchandise, the members of the otaku community did not only read manga and watch anime.[15] As in the case of Japanese otaku, manga and anime fans in 1990s Spain congregated in conventions devoted to their hobbies where they shared their admiration of these genres as expressions of Japanese art. Manga and anime conventions—"salones del manga y el anime in Spain"—were (and remain today) events in which professionals and enthusiasts in the world of Japanese comics and animation could gather. These conventions have served as a means to announce new releases, promote activities such as cosplay and karaoke competitions, and host exhibitions of original works by reputed mangaka and Spanish amateur creators who aspired to make a living off of their hobbies. These sociocultural events also became retail outlets where official and first-edition merchandise of different popular series could be purchased. In addition to official products, the screening rooms at early fan conventions also premiered fansubbed anime not yet officially dubbed or commercialized in Spain. These "salones del manga" marked a milestone in Spanish otaku history, providing a space exclusively dedicated to Japanese comics, animation, and related merchandise.

The First Salón del Manga, el Anime y el Videojuego de Barcelona

Although Salón Internacional del Cómic de Barcelona and Salón Internacional del Cómic de Granada had been running since 1981 and 1994 respectively, the first Salón del Manga, el Anime y el Videojuego de Barcelona took place several years later, October 27-29, 1995. It capitalized on the positive reception of a smaller-scale event called Primera Jornada del Manga ("First Manga Day"), which served as a pilot project on April 22 of the same year in Sant Andreu Teatre, Barcelona.[16] The legendary salon was intended, described, and chronicled as a cultural melting pot that signified a landmark in terms of cultural interaction between Japan and Spain.[17] Even by the standards of those times, the Spanish youth community's fascination with manga and anime was depicted as a "social phenomenon."[18] The following quotation by sociologist and Japanese-language teacher María Dolores Rodríguez included in the event's catalog is very illustrative in this regard:

> The ongoing surge of young Spanish stakeholders in Japanese popular culture could already be referred to as a "sociological phenomenon." . . . A very large proportion of the people who start studying Japanese in Spain have become admirers of its culture before. Throughout these years of teaching, I have realized that, precisely, those who are more motivated and persevere in the study of the language, are the students who study for reasons as simple as: "I feel attracted by Japan; I like its culture"; "I was so impressed by *Akira* that I decided to learn Japanese." These and other similar appraisals regarding popular culture, manga, anime, music, cinema, art and architecture, are recurring themes among the young people who take an interest in Japan.[19]

The catalog created for this pioneering event offers a valuable picture of Spanish consumers' reception and perception of manga and anime at that time, and how the manga "boom" started and consolidated in the early and mid-1990s. The 132-page book contained reviews of popular manga series, such as *Video Girl Ai* (1989-92, *Den'ei shôjo*), *Akira* and *Dragon Ball*, biographies of famous mangaka, such as Nagai Go and Toriyama Akira, historical data regarding Spain's relation with Japan since 1653, and the publication of the best original manga-style comics created by the Spanish participants of the manga contest in different categories, some of whom later became popular manga authors in Spain. Editorials depicted drawing and animation as "fields full of imagination and professional opportunities."[20] An interview in Catalan with Miyazaki Hayao was the highlight of the anime section in this guidebook.[21] Interestingly enough, the word "otaku," which was proudly being used by Spanish fans at that time, had already appeared in a section by Spanish famous comic artist Cels Piñol.[22]

Due to the large influx of attendants, the salon has moved to different locations several times since 1997. To date, the number of visitors is still increasing, with its twenty-third gathering in 2017 registering 148,000 attendees, 6,000 more than the previous year.[23] The long-standing Salón del Manga, el Anime y el Videojuego de Barcelona was the first to take place in Spain and still runs in the fall every year. However, there are other conventions that followed the footsteps of this breakthrough event, such as Jornaicas de Manga, Anime y Cultura Japonesa de Zaragoza (since 1998), Expocomic Madrid (since 1998), I and II Chibijornadas de Manga, Anime y Cultura Japonesa de Marbella (1998), Salón del Manga de Jerez (since 2000), Salón del Manga de Valencia (since 2008), and Salón del Manga de Granada (since 2009) to name but a few.

The Birth of Otaku Associations, Fanzines, and Magazines

In view of the impact of the animated series *Dragon Ball* in 1992, Nuria Teuler (editor and managing director of *Estudio Inu* and *Kame Ediciones* during the 1990s) and Alex Samaranch (CEO of Estudio Fénix, a Spanish provider of publishing services specializing in comics) founded Club de Fans de Akira Toriyama de Cataluña ("Akira Toriyama's Fan Club"). Two years later, ADAM (acronym that translates as "Association for the Defense of Anime and Manga" in English) was established on an electronic messaging network called Fido-Net in response to the relentless criticism put forth by some institutions and mass media outlets that circulated the rumor that manga and anime only addressed themes full of violent content.[24] In July 1998, a group of fans established Asociación Tomodachi, which became the organizer of the first Jornadas de Manga de Madrid (1998) and the well-known Jornaicas de Zaragoza (1998) for several years.

That said, it is no surprise that specialized manga, anime, and Japanese popular culture magazines in Spain have their origins in the first fanzines and mailing lists from the 1990s, evolving into more sophisticated press and electronic formats to date. What seems to have been the first fanzine of its kind started its run in 1993 under the name of *Tsuzu* (later renamed *Tsuzuki*) (Figure 3). Designed to be read right to left as a symbol of authentic Japaneseness, this nonprofit fanzine was the embryo of what subsequently became *Neko*, a popular magazine published from May 1994 to 2000.[25] In 1998, during the fourth Salón del Manga, el Anime y el Videojuego de Barcelona, fans wit-

Figure 3. Full-color cover image for the first issue of *Tsuzu* (1993), the embryo of *Neko* magazine (1994)

nessed the release of the first issue of full-color magazine *Dokan* and, in December of the same year, an analogous publication called *Minami2000* (later simplified as *Minami*); both offered monthly news, reviews, and unpublished material until 2005 and 2008, respectively.

The role of the first nonprofit fanzines such as *Tsuzu* (1993), *Dragon Ball Magazine* (1993) (Figure 4), *Zaragoza Mix* (1997), and *Yamatai* (1999) (Figure 5), as well as the bulletins created, printed, and distributed by otaku associations, was to fill a niche in the Spanish market regarding the dissemination of a growing sociocultural phenomenon. The lack of specialized magazines in an era when the use of the internet was not yet widespread gave the fan sector the impulse to create their own amateur publications.

Figure 4. Cover image of the ninth issue for *Dragon Ball Magazine* (1995).

Figure 5. Founding members of the nonlucrative fanzine *Yamatai* (1999). Photograph courtesy Alessandra Moura.

ADAM's Bulletin Against Censorship

In parallel, some of the otaku associations based in Spain were publishing their own nonprofit informative bulletins, offering reviews of popular manga and anime series and news about their licensing in several European countries, Japan, and North America. At its inception, ADAM listed a total of 33 coordinators and 807 members spread throughout Spain, including some based in Argentina, Chile, Costa Rica, Mexico, Peru, Portugal, and Venezuela, among others (Figure 6).[26] In its "0" issue from June 1997, ADAM's bulletin addressed the subjects of censorship and persecution, collecting signatures in support of the audience's right to read manga and watch anime in Spain.[27] They also held a campaign that provided fans with a list of telephone and fax numbers for several mass media companies to which they could submit their claims and complaints, expressing the nonconformity of the otaku community.[28] The following text regarding this campaign appeared in ADAM's June 1997 issue:

> About two years ago, certain organizations started a smear campaign towards animation originated in Japan "in defense of the spectatorship," based on the "excessive violence" and "attack to moral and family values . . ." and a string of countless such nonsense comments. They have forgotten that what they now call "Japanese cartoons" are the same as those legendary series, such as *Heidi* and *Mazinger Z*, that we were deeply touched by in our childhood.[29]

Significantly, when the above quotation was published, ADAM had already collected eight hundred signatures supporting their petition. Building a robust association with as many members as possible was crucial to achieve their goals; hence they did not hesitate in asking specialized shops to help distribute their bulletin in order to reach fans. As a matter of fact, ADAM's original aim was to protect manga and anime after some extremely successful anime series such as *Dragon Ball*, *Ranma ½*, and *City Hunter* had been censored and removed from Spanish television. Like otaku at the time, the members of ADAM argued that, although these series were being watched mainly by adults, they were also suitable for all audiences:

> They seek shelter under the excuse of children protection when they [adults] are the main and major target of these series. . . . These series, which are obviously suitable for all ages, mainly have an adult audience,

which is being despised by these organizations that consider anime as "just for children," making a big mistake. . . . We claim that censorship has to end, that the associations which claim to defend the rights of the audience are abridging our rights, and that as with any other hobby, we have the right to watch quality anime on television.[30]

Two years later, through its eleventh printed issue, dated April 1999, ADAM prompted the members of the otaku community to send letters and e-mails to audience association Telespectadors Associats de Catalunya, after the latter had sent a formal request to TV2 (Spain's second national state-owned public-service television channel) to remove anime series *Marmalade Boy* (1994) from their programming on the grounds that it was inappropriate for children.[31] It is worth mentioning that *Marmalade Boy* narrates the story of a stepfam-

Figure 6. Cover image of the "0" issue for ADAM's bulletin (June 1997).

ily whose stepsiblings, Miki and Yû, fall in love, and also features a teenage student called Meiko who starts a relationship with one of her teachers. Telespectadors Associats de Catalunya regarded this anime as detrimental for the Spanish young audience, since they considered the family in the show dysfunctional.

As a response to this attempt to remove *Marmalade Boy* from Spanish TV, the twelfth bulletin of ADAM illustrated the VHS tape distribution of fansubbed anime, another action taken by fandom in their efforts to disseminate series that had not reached Spain or were under the threat of censorship.[32] Original anime soundtracks such as *Dragon Ball* and *Marmalade Boy* were also distributed, with full-color covers and some of their lyrics translated.[33] A list of "distributors" was included so that fans could contact them, followed by a note calling for volunteers to contribute in the provision of unpublished material.

The year 1998 also witnessed the mutual collaboration and understanding between ADAM and Asociación Tomodachi, both of which planned to cooperate in the dissemination of Japanese popular culture artifacts in Spain.[34] This issue featured a list of new clubs and associations, too, for the purpose of establishing bonds of fellowship between groups with the same purpose.

On the other hand, ADAM criticized Salón del Cómic de Madrid for not including any manga-related activities in their planning, and for relying exclusively on fans who volunteered to organize the event for free.[35] The disputes between fandom and the industry would become one of the most relevant topics of debate in fan literature.

LCM and MLM: A Meeting Point for Manga Fans and Their Vindication

Lista de Correo Manga (Manga Mail List) or *LCM*, as it was known by fans, was one of the several periodicals that emerged in Spain amid the otaku sociocultural phenomenon during the 1990s (Figure 7). *LCM* was nonprofit, distributed by fans and edited by Jorge Orte, who collected letters from otaku based in different regions of Spain that he would assemble and photocopy to craft the fanzine (Figure 8). The periodical had the same function as contemporary online mailing lists, and in fact an electronic messaging network called *MLM* (Mailing List de Manga) was its embryo. The periodical was developed to reach Spanish fans who did not have internet access at their homes during

Figure 7. Cover image of the 1st printed issue for *LCM* (1997).

Figure 8. Second meetup of *LCM* members. (Left to right) Chiisai (Alessandra Moura), Brahma, Totoro, Shinohara, and Minako. Photograph courtesy Alessandra Moura.

the 1990s, providing them the same content as the original mailing list. *LCM* started its run in 1997, becoming a meeting point for manga and anime fans who sought a place where they could express their opinions about certain manga and anime series, manga conventions and, of most relevance, about publishers.

Surprisingly, the first issue of this A5-size bulletin used the word "otaku" repeatedly, and severely criticized Norma Editorial (Spanish publisher of comics) for the "poor editions and abusive prices" of their manga, memorializing a group of otaku conducting a sit-in at the entrance of the third Salon del Manga de Barcelona as a symbol of protest (Figure 9).[36] They also sent a copy of the fanzine to the publisher, intending to have an impact on the quality of future manga editions.[37] *LCM* also invited publishers to send letters for their publication in the bulletin, and Norma's chief editor Oscar Valiente gave an interview for the fanzine, narrating how he entered the industry because of his fascination with comics.[38] Significantly, the first issue of this periodical also featured a fan who compared the flipping of pages in Spanish editions of manga to the alteration of Diego Velázquez's painting *Las Meninas* (1656) by stating the following:

> Perhaps you are flipping relevant things for the development of the action . . . or maybe not, anyway, you are flipping the masterpiece of an author, thing that I don't think he'd be very pleased about . . . imagine flipping las meninas . . . would you dare?[39]

The 1990s was a decade of harsh fan criticism of the mass media and some of the leading figures in the manga industry in Spain, highlighting the extreme antagonism between the industry and the audience. Nuria Teuler (Kame Ediciones's chief editor) was one of the most severely blamed figures due to her continuous unfortunate comments about Spanish otaku, whom she often belittled during panel discussions at manga conventions, alluding to their eccentric behavior.[40] In response, *LCM* campaigned to ban her from participating in future events, arguing that she monopolized panel discussions.[41] The following extract illustrates fans' response addressing this subject:

> You should already know, Ms. Teuler, that those who sing in karaoke have achieved much more than anyone could expect with even such meager resources. . . . [They have been crucial in] organizing cultural (or subcultural, depending on the point of view) events, putting pub-

Figure 9. Sit-in of a group of Spanish otaku at the entrance of the third *Salon del Manga de Barcelona* as a symbol of protest (1997). Photograph courtesy Alessandra Moura.

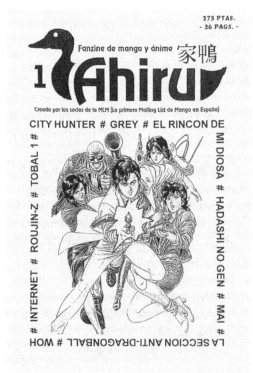

Figure 10. Cover image for the first issue of *Ahiru*, fanzine created by the members of *MLM* (May 1997).

lishers in contact with fans so that both can get to know each other's point of view in an enriching manner and to have a true and well-founded opinion. . . . They have also contacted fans from all over Spain and even from abroad, and everything [has been] non-profit. . . . I just want to clarify that, with this article, I wanted to exert the right of reply that we all have.[42]

The comment above emphasizes fandom's efforts to build a solid community that reached out to publishers to have a voice in the world of manga. At a deeper level, fans defended their right to take part in the decisions taken by the industry and, through their opinions, to become rightful critics of the products they consumed. It is worth noting that, in parallel to their periodical bulletin, *MLM* also edited a fanzine called *Ahiru*, which started its run in August 1997, offering news and commentary about manga and anime (Figure 10).

The Voice of Otaku Regarding Spanish Editions and Translations of Manga

The 1990s also saw criticism regarding Spanish editions of manga. The expensive prices, the poor quality of the paper used in their imprints, and the flipping of pages from Japanese to Western reading formats were discussed openly in fanzines.[43] Likewise, translations were also an object of debate within the otaku community. Despite recognizing the difficulty of the task, many otaku did not seem to appreciate the overall quality of the commercially published translations.[44] In fact, one crucial difference between manga readers and readers of other genres is their critical approach regarding the translations they consume, be they speakers of Japanese or not.[45] Consequently, the otaku community often showed their disapproval towards domesticating strategies in manga adaptations during the 1990s by referring to characters exclusively by their original Japanese names, point that has been recently discussed in translation studies.[46] Spanish manga translations were on the whole rated as "bad," and criticism was often directed toward the adaptations of proper names, as the following extract illustrates:

In the first place, regarding translations, I think that adapting a text from a completely different culture is a laudable endeavor, which can be done more or less correctly, and in some cases, they seem fair enough.

> But most of them slack on many points, such as [the translation of]
> names (let's not make the same mistakes as American editions, please)
> and other practical details I could speak about.[47]

Spanish otaku readership was aware from the 1990s that they were reading
translations and found them intrinsically fascinating. Part of the "genuine-
ness" of manga resided in the fact that the stories depicted were Japanese,
and manga fans expected the translations to give them something that was
as much like the original as possible.[48] Furthermore, fans knew about certain
manga series before they arrived in the Spanish market, and some of them
were already fan-translating popular series in their fanzines. The substitu-
tion of original proper names with Western alternatives was not "believable,"
and consequently was seen as unacceptable and aberrant, a position that per-
fectly matches fans' regarding professional translations of manga "as suspi-
cious, regardless of status" and as an "unwarranted alteration of the original
text,"[49] as the following comment from a Spanish fan who comments:

> If they were just expensive . . . Man! We'd just have to work to get cash,
> but the worst is that they have no idea of how to edit a manga. I think
> that taking a manga, doing a bad translation, making an even worse
> layout, printing it on bad paper, horrible format, without frames . . . is
> not editing. So, we don't have publishers, we have thieves.[50]

Manga readers were unsatisfied with Spanish releases; in this era, they also
sought out editions from overseas despite the challenges involved due to distribution limitations and the language barrier.[51] This illustrates that the phenomenon was not exclusive of *Dragon Ball* series, and in fact otaku in one
division were already purchasing other manga titles in English through the
North American catalog *Advance Comics* almost "blindly" since they "had to
figure out what they were buying just by a cover image and a brief description
in the catalogue."[52] Comparisons among editions translated into different languages were common[53] and, in fact, some members of the otaku community
suggested buying manga in other languages, which they considered better
than the ones that were being published in Spain. As one fan wrote in a letter
to the editor of *Lista de Correo Manga*:

> After this, we can have a look at the wonderful editions published out-
> side of our country and we have two options: we either swallow all this

"garbage" that they try to masquerade as acceptable or "less bad than competitors" . . . or buy them from abroad (guys, learning languages is very handy, I swear, I've done great things).[54]

The extract above could be understood not only as an attempt to acquire manga translated into Western languages. It may also point some manga readers intending to learn Japanese, as Rodríguez suggests.[55] With an understanding of Japanese, fans could access publications in their original versions without relying on what they deemed "bad translations."[56] All in all, the audience of the 1990s had passed from praising publishers for releasing the series they liked to accusing them of doing shoddy work. A comment from one of the members of *LCM* asking that "respect" be given to a community, who claimed to be "fooled" and "ripped off," is just one of the many instances of how frustrated some otaku were with the manga industry in Spain during the 1990s.[57]

From "Otakism" to Specialization: The Intellectual Otaku Infiltrates the Industry

The Spanish otaku community has evolved considerably, with some members becoming connoisseurs of manga and anime, both in the way they are imported in Spain and in their original formats. Influential Spanish figures such as Lázaro Muñoz and Ana María Meca, who started as fans, later became professionals in the manga industry during the 1990s. After several years of participating in manga fanzines and associations, Muñoz founded the well-known magazine *Minami* in 1998, which he regularly filled with editorials about anime and manga. Later, he joined *Dokan* as a contributor. Similarly, Meca explained in an interview that she was actually "a professional archaeologist . . . who had always read comics,"[58] describing how she ended up working for *Neko* magazine and as the chief editor of *Planeta de Agostini* "by accident."[59]

The list of otaku who became professionals in the manga and anime industries is too extensive to recount here. Ferrer, who depicts herself as both "fan" and "translator," dreamt like many other otaku of becoming part of the world of manga in Spain. After starting her career as a manga and anime translator during the 1990s, Ferrer earned a PhD and became an entrepreneur and reputed researcher years later. The following post in her personal blog summarizes her career path, from being a fan to becoming a relevant professional: "Those kids who gathered to create fanzines and dreamt of working in the world of manga during the 1990s will always keep the pride of knowing they made it possible."[60]

Another case in point is Alessandra Moura, a self-described "freak who lives off her hobbies," who declared that she had started her career as a manga and anime translator because she "couldn't stand how they mutilated [her] favorite series."[61] Alessandra Moura was considered a manga and anime activist during the 1990s, participating as a columnist in most fanzines and bulletins, advocating for reliable translations and the preservation of original names of manga and anime characters. She was also the author of *Dr. Slump*'s fan translations from the 1990s and currently continues working in the industry as an anime translator for Netflix. In a personal communication, explaining how she started working as a manga and anime translator, she stated the following:

> The first manga I translated professionally was *Marmalade Boy* by Yoshizumi Wataru. . . . Why did they commission me to do the translation? Because I applied. By then, we all complained about bad translations of anime. I gathered fans' complaints and sent them to Manga Films. When I knew that *Planeta deAgostini* was going to publish *Marmalade Boy*, I asked the Chief Editor (Ana Maria Meca) if they had a translator. . . . I passed the translation test and she hired me. Later, I also heard that they were going to dub the anime so I applied since I was the translator of the manga version. I translated two episodes as a test and the dubbing director (Jaime Roca) commissioned me to do the translation. . . . Since I had all the anime series fansubbed in English by Tomodachi Anime, I could start translating even before they had the tapes in the studio.

The statement above illustrates the scope of fans' complaints during the 1990s and, what is more, how some of them succeeded in entering the industry with the purpose of improving the translation process of these works. The fact that Moura, an otaku and fan translator, started her career in the world of manga and anime is particularly significant since it outlines not only fans' fascination for these genres, and their indignation about the scarcity and allegedly low quality of the commercialized manga and anime in Spain, but also their relevance as active participants within the industry.

Similarly, Annabel Espada, columnist, manga proofreader, and translator, confirmed that she entered the manga industry "by accident" and because she liked it. She started her career at a time "when manga were translated from English . . . by checking that nothing was left behind." Espada was a chemist who started studying Japanese for pleasure in 1997 and ended up becoming *Neko*'s and *Planeta deAgostini*'s chief editor as well as a manga translator. According to Espada, Spanish manga readers do not belong to the "consume and keep quiet type," and she suggests that manga should be edited and translated to remain as close to original versions as possible. She encouraged readers to communicate with publishers, both by mail and in manga conventions, in order to let them know their opinions. Responding to the debate regarding manga reading direction, she acknowledged that Spanish otaku readers have become used to reading from right to left and that, curiously, their complaints are normally about Westernized manga, referring to manga page flipping. With reference to sound effects, Espada considers that they should be kept in the original Japanese kana, especially taking into account that "retouching onomatopoeia implies redrawing" and "modifying the original picture of the creator," something that Japanese authors do not agree with.[62]

Fan scholar Henry Jenkins's analysis is very pertinent in this regard. As he points out, "fandom constitutes a base for consumer activism," as fans assert "their right to make judgments and to express opinions."[63] What is more, every fan is a potential creator "who may be able to make a contribution."[64] In other words, "media fans are consumers who also produce, readers who also write and spectators who also participate."[65] Jenkins's outline of fans as members of an active audience matches Espada's vision on the Spanish otaku. Spanish otaku during the 1990s wanted to read something as close to the original texts as possible, reflecting their conception of manga and anime as original works that should not be altered unnecessarily. This "activism" and "judgment" was, and still is, exerted by the community of fans in Spain, and their creativity and participation in the presence of manga and anime is reflected in activities such as fansubs and scanlations. Fans' wills to preserve as many original features as possible in these works reflect their quest for authenticity and their respect for the artist and the author. Their approach to manga and anime is comparable to the approach taken in the restoration of works of art or the translation of literary masterpieces, where the original intention and personal vision of the artist often become the central axis of the creation. Efforts to enter and interact with the manga and anime industry during the 1990s could be understood as fandom's attempt to highlight the literary and aesthetic value of manga and anime and as a chance to influence the industry from within.

Manga and Anime Two Decades Later

In surveying the origins of the Spanish transnational fandom, scholars often confront a lack of sources documenting the genesis of the phenomenon. In this respect, the surviving fan literature has proven a valuable source to elucidate and illustrate some of the events that took place at the origins of the fan revolution that are generally overlooked.

The Spanish transnational fandom, as can be understood from the fan literature created by the otaku community during the 1990s, played a significant and active role since its inception. Fans were not simple consumers or a mere audience of observers, but participants in a bustling, relevant sociocultural phenomenon centered on the appreciation of Japanese pop culture overseas. Their participation as fans and their critical approach toward the genres they consumed helped raise awareness of manga and anime as valuable artwork rather than being regarded as simple entertaining products for children. The otaku community emerged as a necessity for the anime and manga industry to expand into Spain throughout the decades, especially due to the lack of releases and the urgency to adjust to the audience of consumers. The manga and anime industries received continuous feedback from fandom, which, far from implying destructive criticism, helped trace a path for the successful expansion and reception of Japanese productions. The often-overlooked fanzines and bulletins—predecessors of current Internet forums and blogs—are valuable prisms through which to explore their history in the pre-internet era.

The Spanish otaku community managed to specialize in such areas as conference organization and fan translation at a very early stage, positioning themselves ahead of the industry despite the scarcity of works that reached the country during the 1990s and early 2000s. Some otaku became connoisseurs of these works and even built their careers around their hobbies, infiltrating the market, making the readjustments the community of fans was clamoring for and reshaping the industry. Somehow, the claims of fans were heard and succeeded in preparing the grounds for many of the standards that prevail nowadays: manga pages are no longer flipped, and the names of the characters are rarely Westernized in manga and anime. Spanish releases are much more faithful to their Japanese counterparts than they used to be, and the vast majority are directly based on original artwork instead of relying on pivot editions, a change not only due to the trends introduced through fansubs and scanlations but also thanks to the activism of fans from the 1990s. The demonization of manga and anime by some institutions and mass media critics seem to have ceased, and some magazines, blogs, and internet forums have taken over the fanzines and bulletins that circulated at the genesis of the Spanish otaku phenomenon.

Throughout several decades, the industry has learned to satisfy consumers' expectations, and although the current situation of manga and anime in Spain nowadays might not be flawless, the sought after "authenticity" and current presence of manga and anime in Spain is owed to a great extent to the otaku from the 1990s whose voices still resonate in the twenty-first century.

....

Salomón Doncel-Moriano Urbano has been a PhD candidate at the University of Granada and Visiting Research Fellow at Waseda University since 2017. His research focuses on the impact of the otaku community on the turn-over of professional translation approaches in manga and anime. He has also been contributing to the Spanish industry since 2005 as a manga and anime translator. Some of his most relevant translation works are manga *Your Lie in April*, *Nijigahara Holograph*, and *Koe no Katachi* and anime series *Detective Conan* and *Lupin III*.

....

Notes

1. David Parada Morales, "Manga-Anime: Una Expresión Artística Que Subjetiva al Otaku" (Manga-anime: An artistic expression that subjectivates the otaku), *Tesis Psicológica* 7 (2012): 160–75, http://www.redalyc.org/pdf/1390/139025258007.pdf (accessed February 3, 2018).

2. Rolando José Rodríguez de León, *Los Inicios del Cine de Animación en Japón* (The beginnings of animation cinema in Japan) (Madrid: Adama, 2009), 92–109.

3. Rodríguez de León, *Los Inicios del Cine de Animación en Japón*, 94.

4. Rodríguez de León, 106–7.

5. Jordi Manzanares and Félix López, "Cavall Fort 137/138," *Tebeosfera* (2011), https://www.tebeosfera.com/numeros/cavall_fort_1961_scgvs_137_138.html (accessed January 13, 2018).

6. Annabel Espada, interview by Jordi Querol, *Zona Negativa*, May 1, 2007, http://www.zonanegativa.com/manga/ (accessed October 12, 2017).

7. Josep María Carandell, "Los Cómics Japoneses" (Japanese comics), in *Qué Triste*

Es La Vida y Otras Historias (Life is sad and other stories) (Barcelona: La Cúpula, 1984), 5–7.

8. Ignacio Vidal-Folch, "Planeta Editará en Cómic la Popular Serie Televisiva *Bola de Drac*" (Planeta will publish the comic of the popular television series *Dragon Ball*), *Vanguardia* (Barcelona), January 30, 1992, 31.

9. Genis Puig, "Historia del Manga y Anime 3" (The history of manga and anime 3), *Mision Tokyo*, February 11, 2012, http://misiontokyo.com/articulos/historia -manganime/historia-del-manga-y-el-anime-3 (accessed October 12, 2017).

10. Nuria López Balboa, "*Dragon Ball* Grandes Cambios" (*Dragon Ball* big changes), *Dragon Ball Magazine* 8 (1995), 2–6, 19–25; Alessandra Moura, "Fan translation of Dr. Slump," *Dragon Ball Magazine* 9 (1995), 17–22.

11. Vidal-Folch. "Planeta Editará en Cómic la Popular Serie Televisiva Bola de Drac."

12. Puig, "Historia del Manga y Anime 3."

13. Xavi Ayén, "La Catedral del Cromo se Desborda" (The cathedral of the sticker overflows), *La Vanguardia* (Barcelona), April 1, 1992.

14. EFE, "Requisan a Tres Menores Cromos de *Bola de Drac*" (*Dragon Ball* stickers confiscated from three minors), *La Vanguardia* (Barcelona), March 20, 1992.

15. Heike Elisabeth Jüngst, "Translating Manga," in *Comics in Translation*, ed. Federico Zanettin (Manchester: St. Jerome, 2008), 50.

16. Juanjo Sarto, "Boom del manga," *Catálogo I Salón del Manga, el Anime y el Videojuego* (Catalog of the first convention of manga, anime and videogames), October 1995, 6–11.

17. María Dolores Rodríguez del Alisal, "Encuentro de Culturas" (Encounter between cultures), *Catálogo I Salón del Manga, el Anime y el Videojuego* (Catalog of the first convention of manga, anime and videogames, October 1995, 3–5.

18. Rodríguez del Alisal, "Encuentro de Culturas," 3.

19. Rodríguez del Alisal, 3–5.

20. Yolanda Alonso, "Dibujo y Animación: Campos Llenos de Imaginación y Salidas Profesionales" (Drawing and animation: Fields full of imagination and professional opportunities), *Catálogo I Salón del Manga, el Anime y el Videojuego* (Catalog of the first convention of manga, anime and videogames), October 1995, 98–99.

21. Miyazaki Hayao, interview by Vicent Sanchís, *Catálogo I Salón del Manga, el Anime y el Videojuego* (Catalog of the first convention of manga, anime and videogames), October 1995, 101–5.

22. Cels Piñol, "Otaku," *Catálogo I Salón del Manga, el Anime y el Videojuego*, October 1995, 12–14.

23. Ficomic, "El XXIII Salón del Manga de Barcelona Cierra con Éxito de Participación, Expositores y Mejora de Ventas" Barcelona's twenty-third *Salon del Manga* concludes successfully in participation, exhibitors and better sales), *Ficomic*, November 5, 2017, https://ficomic.com/noticias.cfm/id/30227/esp/

el-xxiii-salon-manga-barcelona-cierra-con-exito-participacion-expositores
-y-mejora-ventas.htm (accessed February 5, 2017).

24. *Boletín Informativo ADAM* 0. Asociación de Defensa del Anime y el Manga, 1997, 6.

25. Genis Puig, personal e-mail communication, July 13, 2008.

26. *Boletín Informativo ADAM*, 0, 12.

27. *Boletín Informativo ADAM*, 2-4, 6-8.

28. *Boletín Informativo ADAM*, 6.

29. *Boletín Informativo ADAM*, 3.

30. *Boletín Informativo ADAM*, 3-4.

31. Europa Press, "Piden la retirada de los dibujos animados *La Familia Crece* de La 2" (Withdrawal of cartoon series *Marmalade Boy* claimed), *El País*, December 4, 1998; *Boletín Informativo ADAM* 11. Asociación de Defensa del Anime y el Manga, 1999, 10-12.

32. *Boletín Informativo ADAM*, 12; Asociación de Defensa del Anime y el Manga, 1999, 2-3.

33. *Boletín Informativo ADAM*, 2-3.

34. *Boletín Informativo ADAM*, 5-6.

35. *Boletín Informativo ADAM*, 5-6.

36. Jorge Orte Tudela, "Les Dio Vergüenza Admitirlo" (They were too embarrassed to admit it), *Lista de Correo Manga* 1, 1997, 15.

37. Tudela, "Les Dio Vergüenza Admitirlo."

38. Oscar Valiente, interview by Andrés G. Mendoza, *Lista de Correo Manga* 1, 1997, 13.

39. Rally, letter to the editor, *Lista de Correo Manga* 1, 1997, 9.

40. Andrés G. Mendoza "!!No Quiero Ser Como Tú!! ¿Es Nuria Teuler la Hija Secreta de Son Goku?" (I don't want to be like you!! Is Nuria Teuler Son Goku's the secret daughter?), *Zaragoza Mix Dos*, 1997, 28-29.

41. Jorge Orte Tudela, "Editorial," *Lista de Correo Manga* 1, 1997, 3.

42. Mendoza, "!!No Quiero Ser Como Tú!!"

43. Rally, letter to the editor, *Lista de Correo Manga* 1, 1997, 9.

44. Iceoff, letter to the editor, *Lista de Correo Manga* 1, 1997, 9.

45. Jüngst, "Translating Manga," 50.

46. Salomón Doncel-Moriano Urbano, "La tradución de *Sailor Moon*" (The translation of *Sailor Moon*) in *Tebeosfera*, tercera época 7 (Seville, 2018), https://www.tebeosfera.com/documentos/la_traduccion_de_sailor_moon.html (accessed September 27, 2018).

47. Iceoff, letter to the editor, *Lista de Correo Manga* 1, 1997, 7.

48. Jüngst "Translating Manga," 60.

49. Kristin Anderson Terpstra, "Spreading the Word: Fan Translations of Manga in a Global Context" (PhD diss., University of Iowa, 2012), 110, http://ir.uiowa.edu/etd/3423 (accessed September 11, 2017).

50. Kuso, letter to the editor, *Lista de Correo Manga* 1, 1997, 8-9.

51. Baeza, letter to the editor, *Lista de Correo Manga* 2, 1997, 4.

52. Alejandro Maicas "Clásicos: *Hadashi no Gen*" (Classics: *Barefoot Gen*) *Ahiru* 1, 1997, 9.

53. Seiji Komatsu, "¡¡¡Qué Mal Traducen Estos Tíos!!!" (These guys translate dreadfully!!!), *Information High*, (n.d.), 23–25.

54. Juan De Dios, letter to the editor, *Lista de Correo Manga* 1, 1997, 5–6.

55. Rodríguez del Alisal "Encuentro de Culturas," 3–5.

56. Kuso, letter to the editor, *Lista de Correo Manga* 1, 1997, 8–9.

57. Baeza, letter to the editor, *Lista de Correo Manga* 2, 1997, 4.

58. Ana María Meca, interview by Andrés G. Mendoza, *Zaragoza Mix Dos*, 1997, 26.

59. Meca, Mendoza interview.

60. María Ferrer, "El Manga Veinte Años Después" (Manga twenty years later), *La Loca Tertulia del Té* (blog), November 11, 2011, https://lalocatertuliadelte.word press.com/2011/11/01/el-manga-veinte-anos-despues/ (accessed November 21, 2017).

61. Alessandra Moura, "La Difícil Tarea del Traductor" (The difficult task of the translator), *Animebaka* 15, February 15, 2002, http://bakaradio.ociologia.org/Animebaka/Animebaka%2015.htm (accessed December 12, 2017).

62. Annabel Espada, interview by Jordi Querol.

63. Henry Jenkins, *Textual Poachers: Television Fans and Participatory Culture* (London: Routledge, 1992), 278.

64. Jenkins, *Textual Poachers*, 280.

65. Henry Jenkins, "'Strangers No More, We Sing': Filking and the Social Construction of the Science Fiction Fan Community," in *The Adorning Audience: Fan Culture and Popular Media*, ed. Lisa Al Lewis (London: Routledge, 1992), 208.

Subtitle and Distribute

The Mediation Policies of Brazilian Fansubbers in Digital Networks

KRYSTAL URBANO

This essay originates from research developed while working on a Master's degree. The objective in that research was to investigate contemporary practices of anime fandom in Brazil associated with the broader sphere of digital networks. For that purpose, I opted to focus on the practice developed by fansubbers and their collaboration system, which consists of translation, subtitling, and the informal distribution of audiovisual products from East Asia—generally anime—in the universe of digital networks.[1]

Emerging from a predigital era, the fansub groups that originated in anime clubs were communities of fans focused on the translation and subtitling of anime. These clubs appeared in the United States by the end of the 1970s with the intention of promoting and spreading anime and other Asian media texts to American fans due to their scarcity in mainstream U.S. media.[2] With videocassette and VHS technology, these clubs went from solely exhibiting videos to producing amateur subtitles. In Brazil, it is hard to give a precise date for the first fansub. As with American fans, Brazilian aficionados built an informal network to trade these animations among friends, acquaintances, and other individuals interested in anime in the 1990s, a network that expanded when it migrated to the internet at the turn of the century. Some fans conferred to BAC—Brasil Anima Club, a group from Brasília founded in 1996—and the title of first Brazilian fansub. The group initially distributed, subtitled, or dubbed material from North American fansubs but later decided to also create subtitles in Portuguese. In this way, fansubbing had evolved in the previous decades by following new technological developments in the reproduction and sharing of files, and has expanded among fans of other countries equally interested in Japanese media productions.[3]

VHS technology made the first amateur subtitling productions possible to a limited degree. More recently, however, using the facilities of the internet and Peer-to-Peer (P2P) communication, fansubbing activity has expanded considerably in terms of mediation and in the use of these technologies.[4] Currently, there are many fansub groups of different nationalities that translate anime into a plethora of languages, in many different versions, making it hard to be precise about the number of groups acting on the internet. Indeed, in recent years the fansubber community has gone from occupying a low visibility, low-impact position in the flux of the global cultural media landscape to a privileged position in the informal, free, and specialized distribution of Japanese serial productions for fans in many countries.[5] This is the case in Brazil, a country where television played an extremely relevant function in terms of diffusion of anime culture to Brazilian audiences.[6]

Certainly, the presence of Japanese audiovisual products in Brazilian media since the 1960s and the migration context that marks the unique relationship between Japan and Brazil are relevant factors behind the emergence of a rising interest in anime among a certain niche of Brazilian consumers in the last two decades. In fact, Brazil is home to the largest Japanese population outside of Japan and Brazilians make up a significant portion of non-Japanese living in Japan (the fourth largest group after Chinese, Koreans, and Filipinos). Therefore, the interest in Japanese audiovisual products became so great in the country during the 1990s that the supply offered by the Brazilian market was not enough to satisfy the demand. From 2000 and onward, this supply of products in mainstream media effectively plummeted because of the new changes in the media landscape that came with the development of the internet in Brazil.[7] For this reason, Brazilian fans interested in Japanese material had to resort to other means to access it. Therefore, fans found other ways of distributing anime through fansubbing practices both physically within the country and in their transposition to the virtual universe. Naturally, the active involvement of these fans, along with the transformations that occurred in the 1990s in social, cultural, economic, and technological fields, created a receptive climate for the transnational distribution of anime, with its own fans as mediators and maintainers.[8]

Considering the technological shift described above, this essay discusses the practices of online anime fandom, focusing in particular on the circuit fed by Brazilian fansubbers and their collaboration system, which consists of the translation, subtitling, and informal distribution of East Asian audiovisual products—usually anime—in the universe of digital networks. With this objective in mind, I develop this argument in three sections. In the first section, I present a discussion of anime fandom as related to contemporary notions such as media convergence, collaborative culture, and collective intelligence. Far from being a community characterized by consensus among its members, the culture promoted by anime fans in their communities involves strong contradictions and divergences. In the second section, I discuss the ethical premises that initially guided Brazilian fansubber activities, in order to demonstrate how the insertion of speed fansubs (groups focused on the rapid translation of new titles) into the fansub circuit promoted a redefinition of the ethos of this fan community. Finally, for purposes of distinction, in the third section I categorize the active and plural politics that guide the fansubbers' collaborative activity, arriving at four axes that, in practice, correspond to ideal types of mediation that guide Brazilian fansubbers. These axes reflect the ways in which subcultural capital and hierarchies[9] within fan community are demonstrated through mediation policies, and propose a more complex conception of the organization of fan collectives.

About Anime Fandom: Between Convergences, Divergences, and Disputes for Subcultural Capital

Fan communities are usually referred to in academic literature by the term *fandom*. This term describes fan collectives centered around a cultural product. In the digital era, both fan collectives and the objects of their interest are usually anchored on the internet. According to Henry Jenkins, one of the pioneers in studies about fandoms, being part of a fandom means overcoming sociocultural isolation through active participation in a fan community.[10] The author recognizes fandoms as collectives that gather around common, shared interests, generating a sense of belonging that may or may not take place through face-to-face interaction. This communal feeling is shared by thousands of fans who not only share the same interests but also value the sharing of experiences, knowledge, and skills. Those interests can refer to any object of desire, be it a musical style or a TV show, but the determining factor of this system is that the relationship established between fans and a cultural text has the same relevance in this new environment. Indeed, the system through which communities of fans organize on the web values the role of a common consumer in the appropriation of certain texts, which form natural starting points and sources of inspiration for multiple re-creations. Fandoms are, therefore, systems of reading and subcultural appropriation or "textual poaching" that can be designated by a group of individuals that share interests, practices, and a system of community driven sense.[11]

Not being the exclusive property of big media conglomerates, contemporary cultural texts are seen as a mix of books, games, music, TV shows, and series that can be freely appropriated by "fans, [who] are the most active segment of the media audience, one that refuses to simply accept what they are given" and who reach for a joint action and/or parallel to the development of fictional narratives by creating new cultural products and by transforming existing ones."[12] As a result, fans have developed practices in their communities that have granted them a new status in the market chain, one that involves globalized cultural production. In that sense, we understand these fans as *produsers*: "produsers mixes the words 'producer' and 'user.' This new concept tries to account for a reality where the word production cannot represent precisely the actual context where the roles of producer and user are delineated."[13] These are active audiences that not only "hunt" for their favorite cultural products, but also act as cultural mediators through the active and affectual consumption of these goods.[14]

The disposition of the fan-consumer for interaction, appropriation, and transformation of cultural artifacts, added to a fast, easy, and cheap means of distributing new content and tools, configures what Jenkins has termed "participatory culture."[15] He elucidates that "instead of talking about producers and consumers of media as occupants of separate roles, we can now consider them interacting participants."[16] In other words, participatory culture is born from an optimistic discourse about the potential of sociopolitical creation and transformation of the common citizen, which emphasizes the many transformations that come from consumer empowerment.[17] It is, therefore, an invitation for fans and consumers in general to produce and spread new contents that have been generated from a matrix or model based on an original product; as imagined by Jenkins, these actions enable a dialog between industries and consumers.

Central to Jenkins's thinking is the idea that sharing knowledge and joining the individual competences of each individual inside their communities of knowledge culminate in the phenomenon of "collective intelligence," a line of thought that originates in the ideas of Pierre Lévy, who suggests that communities on the internet offer "an open field of practice, more participatory, more distributed than those in classic media."[18] That is why, according to Lévy, cyberspace, as a new anthropological space of the permanent construction of knowledge, makes it possible for members of a social group to "coordinate, cooperate, nourish and consult a common memory, almost in real time, apart from geographical distribution and different time zones."[19] By drawing on these discourses of cyberspace, Jenkins supports his argument about the actual constitution of a "collective intelligence" in collaborative practices that emerge in an era of "technological convergence."

Jenkins's concept of participatory culture constitutes my starting point for research on anime fandom. Thanks to the development of electronic communication, the cultural practices of anime fans have also become globalized. Because of that, I follow Nancy Baym and Robert Burnett in arguing that "together, these fans serve as filters of experts as they examine, separate, label, translate, value, and take note of a large, unorganized and geographically remote quantity of these cultural materials for international consuming."[20] In fact, being a fan of anime involves much more than watching anime and consuming them. In its economic aspect itself, it means exchanging knowledge, sharing information, and even developing diverse cultural practices, ranging from painting (fanart) inspired by characters and fictional scenarios of anime to the production of fiction and poems (fanfiction), music videos, films, and amateur dubbing (Anime Music Video, filk music, fanfilms, fandubs), among others. More than that, being a fan of anime also involves discussion and criticism of what is produced both by the official market and within online communities dedicated to anime, among other issues that involve this circuit in the network and out of it. Therefore, these practices allow fans to accumulate not only information but also subcultural capital among themselves.

In Susan Napier's studies of anime fandom based on the ideas of Sarah Thornton, the subcultural capital articulated in communities of anime fans is described as "the knowledge about a certain area of the fandom that enables one to interact with other fans, but also to gather status between its enthusiast colleagues."[21] Therefore, I understand these fans as potential mediators who gain prominence when they become a link between anime (and their derivative subjects) and the other fans in the network. They act as intermediaries in the circuit of this cultural product, forming preferences and patterns of consumption in the course of the activities performed in their online communities. To this extent, they are mediators who gain prominence and singularity in their communities, and who maintain spaces of discussion and knowledge production within the network of eager audiences that make up the larger fandom.

In this way, the demonstration of subcultural capital articulated in anime fandom happens, fundamentally, in conversations about anime, and especially about rare and unconventional cultural products. This incorporation of subcultural capital happens either in the form of "knowing what is needed" to discuss rarer or older productions and, therefore, enter into the fandom circuit as one who is in the loop about rarities, or through news about upcoming shows or the fashion of the moment, related not only to anime but also to Japanese pop culture as a whole. It becomes, then, a matter of considering those attributes and knowledge as reflective of the authenticity of the cultural product.[22] Those who demonstrate a thorough knowledge of their fan object and their fandom's cultural practices are elevated above those who do not possess the distinctive knowledge of a "true fan." So, although some part of anime fans' knowledge capital comes from positive notions about sharing passions and common objectives, it is equally possible to accumulate that knowledge by means of competitive and antagonistic relationships.

A recent contribution that can help better explain the practices shared among anime fans in Brazil and around the world is located in the notion of transcultural fandom. According to Bertha Chin and Lori Hitchcock Morimoto, though there has been a significant increase in the discussion of the term *transcultural fandom*, for these authors, "there is little agreement on what precisely constitutes 'transcultural' fandom."[23] Chin and Morimoto locate a conception of transcultural fandom in Ien Ang's classic work on the reception of the American television series *Dallas*.[24]

> [There is a need] . . . to take seriously not just the national, but also—especially—the gender, sexual, popular and fan cultural contexts within which fans consume and create, if we are to comprehend how and why fandoms arise almost regardless of borders both geographical and cultural.[25]

Thus, Chin and Morimoto understand transcultural fandom as a term with multiple axes beyond the national, a heuristic that can be used to explore a wide variety of fan practices (and objects) found at the boundaries between the community and the global. In the same direction, Sandra Annett affirms that transculturalism is configured in the cultural dimension of transnationalism, in which the idea of nation is replaced by culture.[26] Therefore, instead of emphasizing the eminently transnational character of the fandom of anime, Annett also opts for the term "transcultural," thus understanding that

> [a] "transcultural animation fan community" can thus be defined as a group in which people from many national, cultural, ethnic, gendered, and other personal backgrounds find a sense of connection across difference, engaging with each other through a shared interest while

negotiating the frictions that result from their differing social and historical contexts. In this light, animation fandom is (to paraphrase Jenkins) more than just a marketing concept, but less than a utopian semiotic democracy. Rather, it is a way for people to negotiate the opportunities and challenges of the global media environment that is emerging today.[27]

Building on these surveys, it would be most productive to consider the intersections between national cultures and their practices. In that sense, anime fandom and its correlated practices—like fansubbing and scanlation—cannot be analyzed solely under the spotlight of collaboration and collective intelligence, as Jenkins suggests in the "most politically relaxed phase of his career," according to João Filho.[28] Far beyond configuring a circuit characterized by consensus between its members, the culture promoted by anime fans in its communities involves strong contradictions and dissensions. Fundamentally, I posit the strong existence of hierarchies, alliances, and rivalries that constitute the organization of some of these communities—as is the case on Brazilian fansub groups—which can overlap, generating the dynamics that could lead to the formation of a collective intelligence.

Between Fansubs and Speed Fansubs (and Reencode Sites)

Jihox, a student from Rio de Janeiro, suggests:

> The activity of a fansub has a nice slogan: "From fans, to fans." This is a phrase well known and has some implications, the first one being gratuity. One who commits to developing the fansubber activity, whatever it is, should do it for free. Donations should come from people that feel comfortable contributing to your work in some way and this contribution MUST BE USED to maintain and augment the group's infrastructure, not for the group's enrichment. The other principle [that] is implicit and [that] I like to emphasize is that gratuity shouldn't be an excuse for a bad job. Do the work, do it for free and do the best way possible, ALWAYS. One who doesn't agree with that, don't do it, there are other ways to help that don't involve such commitment. The third practice that I like a lot is that you shouldn't mingle in other group's

business. I will give my opinion about some groups if I'm asked about them, but I won't be "sowing evil."²⁹

Jihox presents an interesting conception of the ethical codes that permeate the fansubber's conduct in anime fandom. In my analysis, the quote above can be used as a good illustration of the traditional ethos still latent in the Brazilian fansubber community. It is a fundamental premise to produce work for fans and any "gratuity" or compensation must be freely given, not demanded, and must be used to support future work rather than commercial gain. Another fundamental value, according to Jihox, is to produce quality work, regardless of receiving compensation or not. Regardless of his strong opinions about the first two principles, and despite the fact he will state opinions about other working groups, the third principle shows that he is unwilling to attack other amateur groups based on these concepts. His third principle grants each group the autonomy to conduct business as they prefer.

Jihox points out the existence of certain ethical premises, values, and hierarchies that represent a traditional system of organization to which the fansubber community has historically and socially adhered since its emergence. Historically, the fansubber community grounded itself in an essential motto that was meant to guide the activity of the groups and its members on anime fandom: "from fans, to fans." More than a motto that shows the selfless character of fansubber activity, it demonstrates the existence of a traditional ethos constructed by the fansubber community that was used until recently to regulate the relationships and actions of the members of this community during its collaborative activities.

If the collective ethos of the fans was historically defined by these premises, however, this community changed in a short period of time because of new social, cultural, and technological circumstances. Indeed, these new practices, the new social actors and politics that emerged in this new environment, demonstrate how the ethos of the fansubber community—being historically and socially constructed—is naturally susceptible to the effects of mutability over time. In fact, some of the main questions revealed by subjects during these interviews and participant observations point to the establishment of new and divergent ethical premises promoted by speed subs and reencode sites that attest to the increasing level of dispute and conflict in this community.

However, the environment of this fan community is a bit more complex than what was ideally imagined. Brazilian translation groups are now divided into two fundamental groups: *fansubs* and *speed fansubs*. Fansubs are firmly centered around the traditional ethos, anchored in a historical code of conduct that reflects a highly orthodox point of view around the practices developed in their communities. Speed fansubs represent a new ethos that operates under a logic centered on the fast, nearly instantaneous, nature of the facilitation and consumption of cultural products. Though it would be prudent to emphasize that the boundaries that demarcate the activities of fansubs and speed fansubs are fluid and, in good measure, those traditional criteria are concealed in this community as a whole, it is interesting to note the approximations and departures between the two models of mediation conceived in this same fan community.

In the first place, historically, fansubs were not created for financial gain and, therefore, fansubbers have not sold their translated anime or other cor-related products in their virtual domains. For that reason, many groups, like the ones addressed in this research—*Ryussei Fansub, Eternal Animes Fansub, OMDA Fansubs, Sukinime, Seitokai,* and *Anime No Sekai*—place the following statement in their subtitles: "Anime made by fans for fans, don't sell or rent." In general, financial return is not seen as compatible with involvement in this collaborative activity. However, participants for this study emphasized that the current activities of translation groups involve an intellectual and cul-tural investment on the part of its members. In particular, these activities re-quire that the fansubbers themselves often need both symbolic and financial investment from their audience of anime fans, for the maintenance of links, sites, portals, and so on. To minimize expenses, many Brazilian fansub groups ask for donations. Others try to be more attractive through a system that pro-vides better upload/download rates for its users based on their contribution to the community. In extreme and controversial cases, a few fansub group charge a monthly fee for VIP access to subtitled media. In general, the idea is that the community, composed of fansubbers and their online audiences, can collaborate to effectively keep their favorite anime online and, consequently, secure the permanence of a fansub operation.

Second, Brazilian fansub groups usually work on anime that has not yet been licensed in their country. When an anime becomes licensed, the fansub group generally stops subtitling it, although exceptions do happen when the licensee intends to heavily edit the original content without releasing an uncut version, as happened in the cases of *Rurouni Kenshin* and *One Piece*. Unlicensed versions released by fansub groups are meant to propagate new anime titles and open access to material not airing in their countries. One case in particular that illustrates this ethos is the case of *Dattebayo*, an American fan-translation group that ceased distributing *Naruto* when the series was acquired by American distribution company VIZ Media LLC. Likewise, in the same period, a number of Brazilian fansub groups that worked with this title also took the anime down from their online catalogs following the example of the American fans. As *Naruto* was airing on Brazilian TV from 2007 to April 2011, a date that marked the airing of the last episode of its saga on Cartoon Network, some Brazilian groups realized that it was no longer necessary to continue its propagation on the web.[30] However, there are many reasons for fansub groups to start or end a project and the acquisition of the rights by local distributors does not necessarily halt the activities of these groups in their countries.

Ultimately, as the work created by fansub groups is not focused on any sort of profit, there would not be a set date or frequency stipulated for the distribution of subtitled episodes. Understanding that the fansubber practice was described by interview subjects as a form of leisure, an organized hobby, guided by devotion to the cultural product itself, I realized that some criteria gain relevance among traditional fansubs. Mainly, the lack of regular airing schedules among fansubbers reveals an opposition in this community to any logic that resembles the dynamics and the timing of the official market. What differentiates the distribution of traditional fansubs, therefore, resides in the valuing of criteria like quality (visual and textual) in their reproductions, in opposition to the logic of mass-market distribution, as is demonstrated in texts made for the commercial market and, more recently, by groups that use the guiding principle of speed.

The speed fansubs, and also the so-called *reencode* sites, have found themselves swimming upstream in the distribution model described above. Both propositions are characterized by promoting a new model based on speed, the agility of distribution, and the ready acquisition of anime on the web. Both propositions aim for nearly synchronous distribution of anime. While speed fansubs still produce subtitles similar to traditional groups, reencodes are groups formed to replicate and redistribute fansub projects and, primarily, of the groups that act on the speed principle, in order to further propagate Japanese pop culture. The definition that came from Skype discussions with subjects in this research is that the reencode sites do not produce "original" work but rather depend on fansub productions. They require the speed imposed by the speed fansubbers to work properly, as most of the audiences of these groups value the immediacy and agility provided by the speeds.

Naturally, speed is imposed as a competitive tool in the online fan community, and its consequences are being felt within the fan community in various ways. More than amplifying their repertoire of titles and the speed of their releases, the addition of new ways to subtitle and distribute anime has significantly altered the ethos and practices that have grounded the activity since its emergence. Once the priority of speed groups shifts to "agility," issues such as "quality" and "authenticity" (and above all, the writing), as well as associations with commercial practices, naturally wind up subject to discussion, as they oppose, in a certain way, the historical premises that guided this community until recently. Fans have addressed these issues as follows:

> We question the immediacy. We question "Punch," because it was the
> first fansub that blatantly started it. They subtitle fast, they have a lot of
> views, became known because generally take the first fansub released,
> doesn't matter which one, and they even change it afterwards. Punch
> subtitles so fast, has a lot of viewers and a lot of leechers, that want
> anime for yesterday. . . . But the problem is ethical. And their donation
> asked of 700 *reais* [is] used for other ends. (*Anissina Keiko* from *fansub
> Sukinime*) [and] The motto "From fan- to-fan" is a practice followed
> by most serious subs, that aim for anime distribution for all without
> aiming for profit, but this environment has some fansubs that commer-
> cialize it, selling anime, shirts and all types of things that can be char-
> acterized more as Piracy than as fansub. At that point those who are
> most doing it are speedsubs, fansubs that don't care for quality, but with
> agility. As said before I won't cite names and will only say that a great
> example of that is a group that starts with "P" and ends with "unch" . . .
> with their allies from "Project." Those are, as I see, examples of those
> who do not follow this motto. (*Aracraud* from *Ryussei fansub*)[31]

Primarily, I observed that those who have been acting longer as fansubbers are prone to despise the practices of speed groups and reencode sites, which are growing in number and visibility among other anime fans on the web. These commentators believe that the agility made possible by speed subs significantly hurt the guiding codes of the fansubber community. Moreover, the activities from some speed groups constitute the core of the conflicts and divergences that permeate this fan grouping. Terms like "trash subs," "fansubs cancer" and other pejorative language were used to describe speed groups, as in the following example:

With the emergence of many "fansubs" that don't value quality and do sloppy work (or Trashsubs as they are called.) the level of national Fansub quality fell a lot arriving to the current situation where someone learns to use Google translator and "learns to encode" makes a "fansub." Today['s fans] most value speed and a minority prefers to wait a bit more to get quality work. (*ShionTNT* from *Eternal Animes e Ryussei fansub*)[32]

While a minority of my interview subjects showed optimism and/or were less affected by the exponential growth of new modes of production and distribution in the fansubber community, others presented a pretty pessimistic view of the popularization of this practice in Brazil. Most mentioned that the fansubber community feels reduced by the popularization of speed subs and reencoding among other fans. This is, in part, because the new practices and groups do not follow the same traditional codes that composed the community since its own emergence. In order to better explain the disputes between Brazilian fansubbers, I propose a model to classify and analyze the four key political dimensions that shape the discourse on distribution within the fan community.

About Fansubber Policies: Classification and Analysis

In order to explain the complexity of the dynamics between Brazilian fansubbers and, above all, to distinguish *fansubs* and *speed fansubs*, I have utilized the data I obtained from my surveys to categorize the policies of fan distribution into four axes. In practice, the axes correspond to four ideal concepts or major discourses that are of great concern to fans. The four categories are: (1) sociocultural and linguistic policies, (2) quality policies, (3) temporality policies, and (4) distribution and accessibility policies. These axes shall be understood as analytical tools in view of the data obtained (Figure 1).

In the first axis, I list the sociocultural and linguistics policies that guide the constitution of fansubs and speed fansubs. These policies became visible when I observed the member admission criteria used by the groups, especially through the most valued competence among fansubbers in a satisfactory final product in their groups. On the second axis, I explore more specifically how the search for an authentic Japanese experience in the fansubber production process depends on establishing certain quality standards (not only textually

Analysis Categories	Sociocultural and linguistic policies	Quality policies	Temporality policies	Accessibility and distribution policies
Fansubs	Translation as the main and most relevant step in the entire process. Preference for translators who have fluent command of the Japanese language, followed by English. Cultural idiosyncrasies retained in anime text add value to the fansubber's translation. Appreciation of original Japanese audio, conferring "nipponicity" to the sonic-imagery experience of anime.	Social and historical notion of quality constructed by the fan collective. Very particular quality criteria that differ from those applied to the official product. Authentic textual-sonic-imagery experience from anime. Artisanal aesthetics in subtitling, based on the idea of excess.	Temporally discontinuous production and distribution of titles. Voluntary cooperation ethics, characterized by leisure time, equally discontinuous. Opposition to dynamics of production and distribution of official market. Translation, image and subtitling quality, in detriment to agility of access and distribution.	Free access and distribution, via torrent, with active trackers for downloading. Ratio System: "measurement of generosity" (fansubs and users). System financially maintained by user donations (trackers survival). Handmade logic of access and distribution. Predominance of nonlicensed titles that are harder to find, already aired in Japan.
Speed Fansubs	Translation as the main and most relevant step in the process. Predominance of translators who know the English language, but have knowledge about the universe of anime. Process of retranslation of scripts in English. Cultural idiosyncrasies are frequently suppressed in translated texts.	Quality value attached to standardized subtitles and agility in distribution. Quality criteria very near what is expected of an official product (clean). Subtitles are standardized and have simplified aesthetics.	Production and distribution of titles/episodes a few hours after official launch. Value on situating audiences closer and closer to the rhythm of new shows airing in Japan. Distribution agility consumed as a fetish among anime fandom.	Access and distribution usually free, via torrent, with active trackers for downloads. Access and distribution logic closer to official market. Predominance of popular, currently airing anime that are distributed by the fan collective. Joint "market economy" and "gift economy": PUNCH Fansubs case.

Figure 1. Mediation Policies of Brazilian Fansubbers. Figure is adapted from the discussion in Urbano, *Legendar e distribuir*, 2013, 130–50.

and visually but also in terms of agility) for the anime translations that each investigated group was working on. On the third axis, I investigate policies related to temporality, especially concerning the rate at which titles were produced and distributed by the fansubs and speed fansubs. Here, the ideals of quality and authenticity built around this community traditionally come into play, as opposed to a temporal logic of production and distribution centered on instantaneousness, that is, rapid consumption as a contemporary tendency of audiences.[33] Finally, in the fourth axis, I discuss policies that involve accessibility and the distribution of anime subtitled by these groups.

The results of this investigation showed that while fansub groups are firmly centered around the traditional ethos, anchored in a historical code of conduct and possessing a fairly orthodox view around the practices developed in this community, the new groups that act at the speed level in this community of fans represent a new ethos, linked to concepts like agility and web-presence, emerging as the most recent development and attaining a privileged place in this circuit.

Therefore, instead of constituting an ideal, mutually supportive or affective environment in its groups, Brazilian fansubbers are each operating increasingly "in an environment with conflict and competitiveness, marked mainly by the emergence of new technical possibilities for production and distribution, the arrival of new members and new practices that started to compose, consequently, the scope of a significant share of these groups."[34] For those reasons, I argue that there is currently a process of redefinition occurring in the modes of distribution, as the fan community attaches itself, fundamentally, to the trend of growing velocity, modifying the artisanal core that had guided this community until recently.

Furthermore, I contend that the recurrent orthodox outlook on fan culture by academic literature in Fan Studies has traditionally looked at what unites groups rather than what might divide them, demonstrating an inadequate and simplifying conception of fandom that does not correspond to the complexity and dynamics of transcultural fandom, such as that of Brazilian fansub groups. Lévy affirms that "the core and the objective of the Collective Intelligence are the mutual recognition and enrichment of people" and that this happens in a kind of community that "assumes as its objective the permanent negotiation of established order, its language, each one's role, the discernment and the definition of its objects, the reinterpretation of its memory."[35] But for Jenkins, who drew inspiration from Lévy's theories, these new communities that arise in digital networks would be "defined by voluntary, temporary and tactical affiliations, reaffirmed through emotional investment and common intellectual enterprises."[36] Although these notions are particularly relevant concerning the internal practices and dynamics of the fansubber community, I punctuate the relationships established between fansubbers as more ambiguous and conflicted than those described by Jenkins, who, for example, believes that "we are witnessing a convergence inside the brain of individual consumers and its social interactions with others."[37]

Far from being harmonious, the dynamics that exist in the fansubber community reveal the establishment of disputes and tensions among its members, especially when the subject of discussion is other groups and their means of production and distribution. That said, I believe there is a traditional ethos in the fansubber community, similar of the one observed in clubber cultures investigated by Thornton, which would try to affirm subcultural values by means of opposition to a general idea of mainstream or—in the case of Brazilian fansubbers—by avoiding any association with a more commercial and/or professional perception involved in their practices and means of fansub organization and distribution.[38]

I observe at the same time, however, that this orthodox ethos is extremely valued in the fan community, even by members of speed fansubs (as suggested by Jihox), since the fansubs with the most visits (like the speedsubs) also end up getting high rankings and visibility inside the community. Also, I find evidence that there is a pressing desire for some of these fansubbers to take on professional roles, exporting their skills while promoting the amateur distribution of anime through fansubs, as is the case of one of my interview subjects, Chiaki-Senpai, who came to split time between fansub activities with *Seitokai animes* and the online streaming service, Crunchyroll.[39] Other examples include platforms like DramaFever (now defunct) and Viki that, joined by Netflix, are aggregating the intellectual capital of Brazilian fansubbers in the translation and subtitling of its titles for inclusion in the official market. Naturally, the distribution models of Crunchyroll, Netflix, and others like Viki seem to favor the ethos of speed fansub groups (although trying to retain the quality of the works).

Indeed, there is a collaborative feedback process promoted by fansubs and speed fansubs that works through not only fans' donations to the groups but also recognition, by the market or the fan audience, of the individual skills of each agent. Both fansubs and speed fansubs integrate, in a certain way, the yearnings and expectations of a plural fan audience that also presents diverse priorities when it comes to the enjoyment of anime.

Conclusion

The modes of distribution promoted by fansubbers in their online communities illustrate the way in which anime fans and audiences increasingly seek to acquire these productions in Brazil. But, far from constituting an isolated phenomenon, fans' alternative ways of consuming foreign media products lead, above all, to the relevance of new media in the propagation and distribution of contemporary audio-visual productions. The contemporary fansubber community contributes directly to establishing a larger circulation of not only anime but also other television and audio-visual formats like TV dramas, reality and talk-shows produced and shared among East Asian countries, meeting the demand that the official market failed to satisfy. Moreover, through the mediation promoted by the collaborative work developed in this community, many anime titles of various genres, formats, and thematic strands, which would not otherwise reach local Brazilian market, are released for other fans in these communities. Through a particular distribution logic (informal, free and specialized), using the facilities provided by production and distribution technologies, the fansubber practice has changed from an amateur hobby to constitute the main core of anime distribution for Brazilian fans.

Above all, it is important to emphasize that my outlook on this fan grouping was initially based on the concept of an "ideal space," in which participants' interactions were firmly grounded around an ideal and/or traditional ethos marked by the passion for anime. Naturally, this first impression was overturned when I started contacting subjects and conducting participant observation, acquiring information that, at first, was unknown to me. The dynamics that shape the ethos promoted by Brazilian fansubbers are as plural as the objectives and aspirations of these agents of anime fandom. In that sense, the ethnographic research conducted for this study emphasizes the worldviews of each participant about the collaborative practice that they develop, allowing us to grasp the complexities of the micro-relationships between the members of this community.

In addition, I suggest that through the activity developed by fansubbers in their online communities, other parallel voices, languages, sounds, and pop expressions coming from East Asia have begun to figure in the already consolidated circuit of Japanese pop and expanding beyond it in Brazil. For instance, South Korean pop culture, which has become known worldwide through its pop music with the Psy's global hit "Gangnam Style" (2012), had already been discovered by a niche of Brazilians through audiovisual works (mainly K-dramas and video clips) being distributed by fans in the spaces established by Japanese pop culture, especially in the digital environment. In fact, in the second half of the 2000s, "K-pop" and "K-drama" were terms that gradually became known and appropriated by the common vocabulary of anime fans, entering the daily consumption of its participants and the practices that involve the Japanese pop culture in the online environment. From the subtitling practices and distribution of Korean dramas, to the maintenance of websites and blogs on the subject, or in the traditional anime conventions, where fans have started to dedicate spaces for K-pop dancing and singing contests, I perceived the unplanned mediations and cultural exchanges between both cultures in Brazil.[40]

Instead of emphasizing the theoretical assumptions that refer to the dynamics of collaborative culture and collective intelligence, both frequently associated with the practices and discussions around fan culture practices, I proceeded along another path that allowed me to comprehend the meaning of multiple mediations revealed by my informants, who constitute the contemporary fan community circuit. The combination of these divergent proposals shows how this fan community is rich in disputes for status, legitimacy, and subcultural capital. These results suggest that it is time for a new approach to fan studies focused as much on contestation as on communal harmony.

....

Krystal Urbano has both a Master's degree and a PhD in Communication from the Fluminense Federal University (PGGCOM-UFF). Urbano focused her research on the dynamics and practices of the fandom of Japanese animations, from the perspective of Brazilian fansubbers and their policies of translation and distribution of audiovisual contents in the digital network environment. In her PhD, developed research on the impact of pop culture in the Far East, specifically in South Korea and Japan, on Brazil, focusing on fan events, live music shows and parties performed under the pop accent "Asian" in the country. She is the coordinator of the Asian Club-Research Group, which is dedicated to pop culture produced in the context of the Far East countries, and linked to the Graduation of Media Studies of UFF and is member of the RIIAM-Ibero-American Network of Researchers in anime and manga.

....

Notes

1. Krystal Urbano, *Legendar e distribuir: O fandom de animes e as políticas de mediação fansubber nas redes digitais (Dissertação—Mestrado em Comunicação)* (Instituto de Arte e Comunicação Social, Universidade Federal Fluminense, Niterói, Agos, 2013).
2. Sean Leonard, "Progress Against the Law: Anime and Fandom, with the Key to the Globalization of Culture," *International Journal of Cultural Studies* 8, no. 3 (2005): 281–305; Henry Jenkins, *Cultura da Convergência* (São Paulo: Aleph, 2009).
3. Hye-Kyung Lee, "Participatory Media Fandom: A Case Study of Anime Fansubbing," *Media Culture Society,* 33, no. 8 (2011): 1131–47; Karolina Cwiek-Rogalska, Magdalena Holy-Luczaj, and Kamil Łuczaj, "Fansubbers: The Case of the Czech Republic and Poland," *Journal of Comparative Research in Anthropology and Sociology,* no. 2 (2014): 175–98; Zongxiao Rong, "Hybridity Within Peer Production: The Power Negotiation of Chinese Fansub Groups" (MSc diss., Department of Media and Communications, London School of Economics and Political Science, August 2014).
4. Rayna Denison, "Anime Fandom and the Liminal Spaces between Fan Creativity and Piracy," *International Journal of Cultural Studies* 14, no. 5 (2011): 449–66; Hye-Kyung Lee, "Cultural Consumer and Copyright," *Creative Industries Journal* 3, no. 3 (2010): 235–50; Ian Condry, "Dark Energy: What Fansubs Reveal about the Copyright Wars," *Mechademia* 5 (2010): 193–208; Mikhail Koulikov, "Fighting the Fansub War: Conflicts Between Media Rights Holders and Unauthorized Creator/Distributor Networks," *Transformative Works and Cultures* 5 (2010).
5. Hye-Kyung Lee, "Participatory Media Fandom"; Urbano, *Legendar e distribuir.*
6. Sandra Monte, *A presença do animê na TV brasileira* (São Paulo: Ed. Laços, 2010); Alexandre Nagado, *Almanaque da Cultura Pop Japonesa* (Via Lettera, 2007); Cristiane A. Sato, *Japop. O poder da cultura pop japonesa.* (São Paulo: NSP-Hakkosha, 2007); Sonia B. Luyten, *Cultura Pop Japonesa: mangá e anime.* (São Paulo: Hedra, 2005).
7. Afonso de Albuquerque and Krystal Cortez, "Ficção Seriada, Cultura Nacional e Des-Ocidentalização: o caso dos animes" *Contemporânea | Revista de comunicação e cultura* 11, no. 1 (2013): 56–71.
8. Urbano, *Legendar e distribuir.*
9. Pierre Bourdieu, "O mercado dos bens simbólicos," in *A economia das trocas simbólicas* (São Paulo: Perspectiva, 1974); Pierre Bourdieu, *A distinção: Critério social do julgamento* (Porto Alegre: Zouk, 2008); Susan Napier, *From Impressionism to Anime: Japan as Fantasy and Fan Cult in the Mind of the West* (Basingstoke: Palgrave Macmillan, 2007); Sarah Thornton, *Club Cultures: Music, Media and Subcultural Capital* (Middletown, Conn.: Wesleyan University Press, 1996).
10. Henry Jenkins, "When Piracy Becomes Promotion: How Unauthorized Copy-

ing Made Japanese Animation Profitable in the United States," *Reason Online,* December 2006.

11. Henry Jenkins, *Textual Poachers: Television Fans and Participatory Culture* (New York: Routledge, 1992).

12. Jenkins, *Cultura da Convergência,* 131.

13. Axel Bruns, *Blogs, Wikipedia, Second Life, and Beyond* (New York: Peter Lang, 2008).

14. Michel De Certeau, *A invenção do cotidiano: Artes de fazer* (Petrópolis, RJ: Vozes, 1994).

15. Jenkins, *Cultura da Convergência.*

16. Jenkins, *Cultura da Convergência,* 30.

17. Bruno Campanella,"O fã na cultura da divergência: hierarquia e disputa em uma comunidade on-line," *Contemporanea | Revista de comunicação e cultura* 10, no. 3 (2012): 474-89.

18. Pierre Lévy, *A inteligência coletiva: Por uma antropologia do ciberespaço* (2nd ed. Tradução de Luiz Paulo Rouanet; São Paulo: Loyola, 1999), 129.

19. Pierre Lévy, *Cibercultura* (São Paulo: Editora 34, 1999), 49.

20. Nancy K. Baym and Robert Burnett, "Amateur Experts: International Fan Labor in Swedish Independent Music," *International Journal of Cultural Studies* 12, no. 5 (2009): 433-49, 3.

21. Napier, *From Impressionism to Anime,* 150; Thornton, *Club Cultures.*

22. Pierre Bourdieu, *O poder simbólico* (Rio de Janeiro: Bertrand Brasil, 1989); Thornton, *Club Cultures.*

23. Bertha Chin and Lori Hitchcock Morimoto, "Introduction: Fan and Fan Studies in Transcultural Context," *Participations: Journal of Audience & Reception Studies* 12, no. 2 (2015): 174.

24. Ien Ang, *Watching Dallas: Soap Opera and the Melodramatic Imagination* (London: Methuen & Co., 1985).

25. Bertha Chin and Lori Hitchcock Morimoto, "Towards a Theory of Transcultural Fandom," *Participations: Journal of Audience & Reception Studies,* 10, no. 1 (2013): 93.

26. Sandra Annett, "Imagining Transcultural Fandom: Animation and Global Media Communities," *Transcultural Studies* 2 (2011): 173.

27. Annett, "Imagining Transcultural Fandom," 174.

28. João Freire Filho, *Reinvenções da resistência juvenil: Os estudos culturais e as micro-políticas do cotidiano* (Rio de Janeiro: Mauad, 2007).

29. Urbano, *Legendar e distribuir,* 119.

30. Available at http://www.anmtv.xpg.com.br/naruto-finaliza-nesta-segunda-no -cartoon-network/.

31. Urbano, *Legendar e distribuir,* 144-49.

32. Urbano, 139.

33. Paul Virilio, *Velocidade e política* (S. Paulo, Estação Liberdade, 1996); Paul Booth, *Digital Fandom—New Media Studies* (New York: Peter Lang Publishing, 2010).

34. Urbano, *Legendar e distribuir*, 127.

35. Lévy, *A inteligência coletiva*, 29–31.

36. Jenkins, *Cultura da Convergência*, 57.

37. Jenkins, 30.

38. Thornton, *Club cultures*.

39. Available at https://www.crunchyroll.com.

40. Krystal Urbano, *Beyond Western Pop Lenses: O circuito das japonesidades e coreanidades pop e seus eventos culturais/musicais no Brasil* (Tese—Doutorado em Comunicação) (Instituto de Arte e Comunicação Social, Universidade Federal Fluminense, Niterói, Set./2018).

Japanese Exceptionalism and Play Hegemony

The Construction of Ludic Traditions in .
Video Games Criticism

TOMÁS GRAU

In November 2004, Namco decided to distribute the game *Katamari Damacy* for the PlayStation 2 to the American market.[1] The title had not been particularly popular in Japan, but its critical reception was generally positive, and it managed to gather a small cult following thanks to the promotion of both Western and Japanese outlets. Most critics at the time focused on the "quirkiness" and "weirdness" of the game and emphasized the way that its mechanical and visual trappings were not comparable to anything from the market at that moment. In some instances, that uniqueness was partly explained by the assertion that Japanese game designers were no match to anyone in regards of "doing weird."

The premise and objectives of the game are simple enough: as the Prince of All Cosmos, the player's duty is to correct the King's mistakes in rebuilding the stars and constellations of the world by combining as much objects as possible into a singular ball that might eventually become a star. To achieve this, the player needs to roll up a ball with these items and keep adding up as many things as possible before times run out, which establishes the main dynamic of the game. At first, players begin with small items (like rubber ducks, cutlery, and calculators), then shift to medium-sized ones (like furniture), large ones (including people and cars), and finish by adding up entire mountains and buildings. Everything counts so long as you are able to keep rolling.

The creator of the game, Keita Takahashi, explained years later in an interview that when coming up with the design of the game he based it around concepts that "a Japanese person would recognize instantly and that would be fun to play with."[2] This assertion signals a cultural focus during the creative process that may have had a role in the reaction that most English-language critics had of the title. However, it is important to indicate that these cultural specificities were never explicitly indicated by game reviewers at the time;

Figure 1. Screen capture of a typical game session in *Katamari Damacy* (Namco, 2004), in which the player has already amassed a significant ball.

instead, they opted to focus on the alienating effect that the game had on them. To these critics, the most attractive aspect of *Katamari Damacy* (Figure 1) and its sequels had less to do with its cultural point of origin than with its presentation as something unique and different from any other game.

What led reviewers to react so strongly toward *Katamari Damacy* was a combination of technical, historical, and cultural factors. The game was received during a time of diversification in the gaming hardware industry that significantly altered the structure of the sector. Nintendo DS was also released in 2004, and marked the beginning of a significant shift in Nintendo's business strategy toward reaching a more diversified market. Last, this year also marked the public release of the digital platform Steam, which has had an enormous impact on the distribution of the industry.[3]

These technical and economic factors had a significant influence on the material conditions in which games operate, both as commodities and as works of art. They also determined which types of genres and experiences would be favored by investors and players alike, which in turn left a mark on the artistic development of the medium. For these reasons, the idea that *Katamari Damacy* was "weird" or "quirky" was an implicit recognition that its play experience was outside of the cultural landscape that these factors promoted. Instead, the game had to be described on its own terms, without fitting it into existing categories and genres. *Katamari Damacy* was not an exceptional case; difficulties describing games considered "bizarre" and "weird" for the mainstream audience are a relatively common situation with titles that deviate too much from the norm. This habit of coupling "difference" with "weirdness" in video game criticism has given many Japanese games a reputation as both singular and engaging experiences and has dictated the treatment of entire game genres, such as visual novels, for years.

Ever since the massive assimilation of Japanese pop culture in Anglophone countries, "Japaneseness"—or even the existence of Orientalism as a recognizable cultural practice— has become increasingly difficult to properly assess. While Anglocentric perceptions and articles dedicated to Japan- or Asia-bashing are still common, today's popular culture has developed around transcultural traits and communities that transcend both local boundaries and simplistic representations of "us" and "them."[4] Such hybridization has been particularly successful in avenues like the gaming and toys industry, which has managed to produce commodities that cater to Asian, North American, and European audiences alike. From popular toy lines, like the ones produced by Takara and Bandai, to digital games like those developed by Nintendo, Sony, and Sega, the transnational appeal of Japanese popular culture has been a reality for decades.

The apparent success of Japan's cultural industry has also been seen by some commentators and analysts as an indication of the Japanese business sector being "ahead of the curve" in cultural trends, a success that has fostered a very particular form of national pride.[5] In that regard, it is interesting to highlight that *Katamari Damacy*'s success came not long after Douglas McGray's infamous article on Japan's "gross national Cool" and the passing of the Basic Law on Intellectual Property by the Diet, which was based on the premise that the future strength of Japan would depend on its ability to "brand" itself as internationally attractive.[6] Since its conception as a cultural policy, the attempts at making Japan "cool" have been deployed with variable success: though some of them have been absorbed and internalized by audiences and consumers at large, other have been met with various degrees of resistance. In that regard, Japan's perception as a "subempire of signs" within

Asia has quickly vanished in favor of a more complex, transnational regional-ism that includes the input of several countries and communities that spread around the globe in different ways.[7]

Nowadays, the complexity revealed in our cultural commodities has reached a point where it is no longer possible to apply any kind of national boundary to these objects, and it becomes more useful to treat them as trans-national products in scholarly inquiry. Alongside this process, however, binary conceptions of Japan as either "cool" or "weird" continue to permeate popular discourse in Anglophone and Hispanic countries.[8] In lockstep with the evolution of the Japanese "brand" itself, the Japanese gaming industry is portrayed today either as a hub of innovation and creativity that shares its brilliance with the world or as a decaying and almost xenophobic market that barely consumes anything outside a very limited range of gaming "genres."[9] Such contradicting depictions have not gone unnoticed by Japanese compa-nies and designers, who have claimed on more than one occasion that their industry needs to cater to "Western" tastes to stay relevant.[10]

With these priorities in mind, the popular Japanese gaming magazine *Famitsu* released a survey that asked non-Japanese players what elements of Japanese games they enjoyed the most, with the assumption that those results could provide guidelines for Japanese studios to maintain their influence in the future.[11] The answers obtained (and the nature of the question itself) are useful to question the kinds of images that Japanese videogames transmit to so-called Western audiences. Beyond that, it reveals some deeply stereotyped conceptions about Japanese games in particular, and Japan in general, that deserve deeper critical examination.

Constituting Identity and Otherness in Gaming Culture

Traditionally, "weirdness" and "bizarreness" are denotative terms that, when found in any text regarding Japanese games, convey a sense of Otherness to very specific elements of the object itself. Unlike other terms, these words are highly specific in their definitions and tend to be used only to encapsulate a small portion of the overall text. They also suggest a distinction between what is considered normal in the game to the observer and what is not. This denotation assumes that, whatever the country of origin, some aspects of game design are more "universal" than others. It also implies a disposition on the part of the observer to assume "universality" in every text they may find and, because of that, the presence of anything remotely different is treated as shocking and even traumatic. This mindset, it follows, assumes the existence of commonalities between Japanese and Western players and developers in aspects like taste, gameplay preferences, and even playing habits. The presence of "weird" titles is considered, in a sense, an act of open defiance to this hegemonic conception of gaming and, in terms of game design and audience engagement, a conscious break from tradition.

As defined by historian Eric Hobsbawm, a "tradition" is a collection of practices usually defined by rules that aim to enforce a set of behaviors and values through the repetition of those practices, with the purpose of establishing a link to the past by way of honoring them.[12] Like similar terms from the field of Cultural Studies that describe the social milieu of a group, its connotation implies a sense of active practice on the part of the individual. Likewise, "tradition" codifies the cultural and social expectations of the group with regards to certain social forms. To be part of a tradition, whether it comes from institutional sources or from well-settled customs, is to embody the rules and norms that govern the material conditions of a specific subset of existence.

When applied to the act of play and the constitution of playing habits, this process of embodiment is tacitly accepted by game scholars of different strokes. On the one hand, psychologists like Lev Vygotsky have suggested that play constitutes a transitional state during the cognitive development of the child, who learns through games how to both correlate meaning with specific signs and imbue objects with it. On the other hand, authors like Janet Murray have theorized the possibility that games play a significant role in shaping the human mind and culture during its nascent state, an observation that is itself an extension of the assertion made by Johan Huizinga about humans "playing" culture. For all these authors, games and play are causative elements that precede the shaping of the human mind and the development of social practices that, through reaffirming repetition, wind up becoming "culture." In this process, these practices become "hegemony" and "tradition" in the sense that they become accepted modes of behavior, which are associated with a fixed number of persistent values. The act of playing a game with a mindset that differs from normatively settled behavior can become an act of transgression and a gateway to experience other ways of interpreting and participating in society. It can become, therefore, a way to experience other experiences and, to a lesser extent, embody a sense of Otherness.

In the digital games market, this feeling of perceiving the Other is manifested through acts of consumption. As anthropologist Anne Allison has argued, Japanese culture provides many fantasies and desires that are shared by a global audience, which helps to establish communities across the world through affective relationships around certain Japanese games.[13] These shared properties have also developed a uniform language of engagement across media landscapes, one that is mostly incentivized by the business strategies of a select number of transnational corporations. It also has a clear effect on designing games. Numerous works have highlighted the formal qualities shared among Japanese, American, and European video games, and assign Japanese games a primary role in shaping up those qualities during the formative period of the medium.[14] This appraisal can be partially explained by the fact that, in the last thirty years, all video game firms have become more financially intertwined. However, it also reveals that Japanese games have garnered international prestige through well-established communities of fans whose discursive praxis eventually filters into mainstream "gamer" culture.

Sociologist Pierre Bourdieu posits that groups with different cultural capital develop different interests and trends between them, which mediates heavily on the kind of objects that they tend to prefer consuming.[15] This perception, therefore, puts the emphasis on circulation as the main means toward the creation of taste and of cultural imaginaries. Using this lens, the perception and distinction of Japanese videogames is one that emerged after the establishment of fan communities that asserted themselves through access channels like gaming magazines in the late 1970s. From that point forward, the appreciation of Japanese games has been relatively constant in Western media, with several titles being highly praised by critics and academics alike. This includes franchises, individual titles, and the overall output of companies like Sega and Nintendo. The rise of Japanese games is commonly associated with the beginning of the popularization of the medium itself by journalists and historians, which Koichi Iwabuchi has argued can be attributed to a conscious "deodorization" strategy on the part of Japanese contents companies.[16] This strategy is best exemplified in the supposed presence of *mukokuseki* ("stateless" or, in Iwabuchi's words, "odorless") aspects in hit Japanese media, as opposed to marginal ones that have much more limited scopes. Examples like *Katamari Damacy* should show us that mukoseki is not necessarily a mark of overseas success, but it can nevertheless be used as a description of those Japanese games that, for one reason or another, have resisted the label of "Japaneseness."

Currently, the most significant gaming markets are not necessarily delimited by spatial or geographical boundaries (as they used to before the advent of digital distribution) but by the content and images that their audience shows a preference toward. The capacity that some Japanese texts have had to cater to several of these preferences at the same time is seen as an indication of Japan's success. The less popular a product is, logic dictates, the more it can be attributed to its lack of international appeal. Cases like *Katamari Damacy* show that, sometimes, games succeed precisely because of their perceived "Japaneseness." Critics, however, do not always take into account the complexities and nuances of the material and the social conditions that foster the development of some Japanese games, and oftentimes, they tend to resort to highly objectified descriptions of Japan. The success of Japanese popular culture in the West, both in video games and other cultural forms, may allow for a greater diversification of categories, but those same classifications are still being highly influenced (if not determined) by an Orientalist gaze that overtly simplifies the internal processes of Japanese culture.

Recently, authors such as Jérémie Pelletier-Gagnon, Martin Picard, Antonio Loriguillo-López, and Víctor Navarro-Remesal have attempted to establish Japanese games as a specific category of study within game studies (called *gêmu* in honor of the Japanese expression), in the belief that such categorization might offer better insight about the local processes that affect Japanese games from their inception.[17] This demarcation is indeed useful to clarify some internal factors that might have been otherwise neglected, and it opens up the possibility to distinguish which typical features of Japanese games are treated more familiarly by critics and players and which ones are considered abnormal or "weird"; in other words, which elements in Japanese games are included in the ludic tradition of the consumers and which ones are excluded.

The framework used to ascertain this distinction is that of constitutive rhetoric, as originally defined by Maurice Charland and recently applied in the field by Mia Consalvo and Christopher A. Paul.[18] According to the interpretation of Consalvo and Paul, constitutive rhetoric in gaming pertains to interpellations about which games are "real" and which are "fake," a rhetorical device that conforms entire groups of people from across separated geographies and enables them to find commonality through messages (whether from ad campaigns or by prominent figures in the community) targeted at their identity. In practice, this process of identity construction establishes beforehand the typology of games that will be considered legitimate by that group and the intensity of attention that will be given to them. What this process entails is twofold: first, it establishes a stark separation between "legitimate" and "illegitimate" play habits and types of gaming. Second, it establishes a hierarchy between "preferential" game genres and "inconsequential" ones. Preferential types are assumed to hold a bigger importance for the overall advancement of the medium while inconsequential ones are usually labeled as "niche" or even "old-fashioned."

The influence of these rhetorical devices in both gaming culture and game studies is evident, according to Consalvo and Paul, in the way that media outlets like Kotaku and Gamasutra, as well as academic journals like *Game Studies* and *Games & Culture*, tend to focus on certain sectors of the medium while leaving others entirely out. It should be noted that, while they do not specifically address whether these practices reflect fan practices as well, they assume a certain reciprocity by stating that communities are encouraged to "identify with or against a group, which furthers a process of dividing and targeting members of particular communities."[19]

Although Consalvo and Paul mostly focus on so-called game genres and general labels such as "realness," "fakeness," "hardcore," and "casual," their methodology can be applied to any aspect within a game, including mechanics, aesthetics, and even authorial background or a game's "pedigree," which Consalvo and Paul acknowledge as potentially of great importance. The assignment of "Japaneseness" to Japanese titles works in a similar way, albeit with some remarkable differences. As Pelletier-Gagnon posits,[20] "Japaneseness" is mostly constructed by the "interpretative" community and by the structures that allow the circulation of Japanese games. Depending on the fan community and the means of circulation (for example, whether the game has been officially translated or not) the intensity of a game's reception varies significantly and, with it, its significance as either a "cool" or a "weird" title.

Another fact that needs to be considered is the implication of several Japanese games with the Japanese media mix itself. This relationship can be found in their shared qualities and aesthetics, which are highly itemized by Loriguillo-López and Navarro-Remesal[21] and can be especially telling in game genres like the visual novel. Many of the elements highlighted by these authors, like "mascot culture," "animation techniques," and "kawaii aesthetics," are similar to the ones offered by participants in the survey that was recently launched by *Famitsu*, and certainly reveals a correlation between certain elements of Japanese games and the reason why some players are attracted to them as a whole.

However, describing those cultural forms as if they could only be found in Japanese texts is not accurate in the least and, even when they are present, their perception as essential signposts of "Japaneseness" is put into question when we consider that they are very historically contextual elements. Instead, it is better to equate "Japaneseness" with the elements and aspects of any video games that, due to discursive circumstances, are considered "external" or "Other" to the "universally shared" conception of the medium.[22] The elements categorized by Loriguillo-López and Navarro-Remesal are present in multiple game geographies, especially in independent titles that make use of similar software tools or resort to the same fantasies that Japanese designers evidently prefer. A particular example of this is the proliferation of games based on popular software tools like RPG Maker, which, despite its origin in the Japanese dôjin games scene of the mid-1990s, has garnered a progressively more global user base over the years.[23] Although it is possible to isolate and assign specific signs and elements of game design to a Japanese point of origin, it is the way that they are received and circulated that determines their "Japaneseness" in any given cultural context. Thus, I propose that, during an interpretative process, a sense of belonging and of being part of a certain "tradition" is evoked by "gamers" to assert which one of their consumption practices and aesthetic sensibilities are considered "real" or part of their tradition, and which are not.

Case Studies: *Intelligent Qube, Katamari Damacy,* and *Metal Gear Solid 4*

Based on this methodological framework, I analyze the critical reaction of three specific case studies to determine which of their elements were assimilated into the ludic tradition of certain media outlets and which become Otherized. One main vector to consider in these cases is whether their game design follows explicitly mukokuseki patterns, which means that we need to ascertain whether the game is attempting to cater to non-Japanese players or if it is only aimed at a local audience, partly by considering Japanese perspectives on the game: for instance, whether the title received any sort of recognition from Japanese media outlets or acknowledgments from public institutions. These games' degree of "mukokuseki-ness" will be potentially enhanced in future research by adding the reception of Japanese media outlets and fan communities as well, and by determining if their impact have followed similar patterns.

Considering all these elements, I focus on three titles, all of which met with varying levels of success in international release, showing how the interpretative community surrounding Anglophone gaming subcultures determined the perception that players had of each title at the time. The games are *Intelligent Qube, Katamari Damacy,* and *Metal Gear Solid 4: Guns of the Patriots.*[24] All were featured in the Japan Media Arts Festival as Jury Selections and, in the case of *I.Q.* and *Solid 4,* were awarded an Excellence Award as significant contributions to their artistic field. The game that best exemplifies mukukoseki strategies is *Metal Gear Solid 4,* as it implicitly avoids any sort of cultural reference in its conception, while *Katamari* is at the opposite end of the spectrum due to the direct inspirations it takes from Japanese culture. *I.Q.,* on the other hand, is a prime example of a highly hybridized game that includes both mukokuseki and non-mukokuseki elements: despite belonging to a relatively "a-cultural" field of design sensibility, it is still treated as a "niche" title that only certain kinds of players may appreciate.

After setting the framework, we proceed to analyze the reactions and descriptions offered by critics during the time of their release in American and European markets, as well as the ones provided by the Japanese Media Arts Festival. In the case of *I.Q.,* the game won an Excellence Award because its "skillfully planned plot juxtaposes the fear of falling against the strategy and planning required to win."[25] The premise of the game is based around clearing rows of cubes that approach the player's avatar in a placeless platform: the player needs to mark specific spots on the platform, wait for a cube to slice into them, then deactivate them and make the cube disappear (Figure 2). While it is possible to do this with every single cube, the objective is to wait until certain cubes are aligned to clear them in one stroke, incentivizing strategic planning.

Game critics from game magazines and web outlets like IGN, Gamespot, and Electronic Gaming Monthly gave *I.Q.* fairly high scores, although they tended to agree that the game would only be appreciated by a small audience. Of all these titles, only the Gamespot review mentioned its country of origin by comparing it to *PaRappa the Rapper,* another game that was considerably popular in Japan but found only a small audience abroad.[26] The reviewer explained that due to the nature of the genre (puzzle games), the game was doomed to obscurity relative to other Japanese titles of the moment like *Final Fantasy VII.*[27] The review concluded that the game was a "good original puzzle game" and therefore meant for a small audience. Later reviews of the game's sequel called it a retroactive "breath of fresh air" that avoided the "top-down 'Tetrisisms' that most other puzzle games clung to."[28] Outside of these reviews and events, the *I.Q.* franchise itself has never garnered too much attention from fans of either gaming culture in general or Japanese games in particular,

Figure 2. Screen capture of one of the puzzle stages of *Intelligent Qube* (Epics, 1997)

lacking a notable footprint on sites like YouTube. The game itself is usually lumped together with similarly obscure titles made by the same studio, like the *Yarudora* series.[29]

The reviews of *Katamari Damacy* employ similar language and references to its "unique" and "bizarre" nature. While praising its "creativity" and "originality," they also assigned it a "cult classic" status, asserting that its chance of success would be limited. Jeremy Parish went so far as to predict that "*Katamari Damacy* is probably not a game destined for major success," which as it happened was completely incorrect.[30] Arguably, in the case of both *Intelligent Qube* and *Katamari Damacy*, critics and players' lack of expectations for the game was a factor in the positive reception they initially garnered in games media. Over the years, the *Katamari* franchise also became popular enough to attract fan production, such as music remixes and other fanworks. One example is the Katamari Collection Twitter account, a bot that posts every item description of the original title. Mondo's independent release of the game's soundtrack on vinyl and Boss Fight Books' recent release of a dedicated volume[31] reveal that interest in the game has not only persisted over the years but might be even expanding.

The last case study, *Metal Gear Solid 4: Guns of the Patriots*, was released with great fanfare in America and Europe to almost immediate worldwide critical acclaim (Figure 3). Unlike *Intelligent Qube* and *Katamari Damacy,* the bulk of the reviews contextualized their critique vis-à-vis other titles in the *Metal Gear* franchise and treated the game as a continuation of the franchise's distinctive design and aesthetic elements. Reviews also championed it as a major reason to purchase a PS3 and claimed it as proof of lead designer Kojima Hideo's artistic achievement.

By the time the game was released, the franchise had become one of the most revered in the world. Part of this affection came from the fact that *Metal Gear* was acknowledged as a progenitor of the "stealth genre," a category popularized thanks to titles like the original *Solid,* which is usually characterized by a mixing of reflexes and cogitation that encourages hiding and experimenting with different kinds of objects to distract or get rid of the guards that populate the play space.[32] While these aspects of the play experience are the ones that most players tend to recognize when they talk about *Metal Gear,* many others are also attracted to the narrative component of the series, which is well known for being extraordinarily complex and thematically rich, usually dealing with hot-button contemporary issues like privacy, the military-industrial complex, the legacy of the Cold War and nuclear deterrence, and the influence of social media on the individual.[33]

Affection for the franchise online dates to 2001, when fan webpage *Metal*

Figure 3. A screen capture of a player as he sneaks behind a guard and avoids detection in *Metal Gear Solid 4: Guns of the Patriots* (Kojima Productions, 2008)

Gear Forever was first published, which itself was predated by the franchise's appearance on Fanfiction.net, where fanfiction for the franchise had already been posted in 2000.[34] By the time *MGS4* was released, years of continuous fan dedication had cemented its place as one of the most revered texts in the medium.

Ironically, the popularity of the franchise allowed for a more varied and ambivalent reaction to the title than *I.Q.* or *Katamari Damacy*. Some outlets were lukewarm at best, with negative comparisons to the previous title in the franchise, *Metal Gear Solid 3*.[35] For these critics, the main problem came not so much from the game but from the franchise itself, which they considered unsatisfactory when compared to similar works at the time, like *Pandora Tomorrow*.[36] Other critiques, like the one by Edge, were negative about the game's nostalgic treatment of previous titles in the franchise. Nevertheless, the reviews were largely positive overall, and even small complaints generated a great deal of controversy.

Game critics at the time were familiar with the kind of experience that the game was going to offer; the franchise had already been assimilated into the ludic tradition of most Anglophone gaming communities, unlike *Intelligent Qube* and *Katamari Damacy*, so critics and academics were better able to generate a more nuanced perspective on the franchise. *MGS4* was largely treated with admiration and respect by fans and critics alike, as it was already part of a beloved franchise.

The citation for the Media Arts committee's Excellence Award stated that on *MGS4* "the team was able to realize a lively game through a new dimensional cinematic image."[37] To the committee, the chief artistic triumph of the game was its overall contribution to the medium, not its impact within Japanese gaming culture. Their willingness to elevate the game above its local context was slightly hampered by the fact that the franchise had already been exoticized in previous years because of some perceived idiosyncrasies, especially in preceding titles. For instance, the first title introduced a sequence where the player needed to switch controller ports in order to fight a seemingly omniscient metahuman. At the time, these differences were taken as part of the authorial intent of the franchise's main designer, Kojima Hideo. As such, descriptions of the franchise adopted a theoretical model similar to those applied to other media, namely auteur theory. Much like its filmic and literary counterparts, this value system enabled critics to assign every quirk of the franchise to the will of a specific author, a treatment that had already been applied before to Japanese designers like Miyamoto Shigeru and

Suzuki Yû. It also is, as Consalvo and Paul show,[38] a common dynamic found in gaming culture that helps consumers and critics recognize the perceived significance of some gaming titles over others.

All three of these games were highly praised by critics. However, their reception was markedly different. While well-established affection for the brand allowed *Metal Gear* to have a major impact on the market, the design of *Intelligent Qube* and *Katamari Damacy* meant they were perceived as niche or cult titles. *Qube's* similarities with previous games like *Tetris* eventually became useful rhetorical tools that critics used to establish some commonality between the title and the category of "puzzle games." It also allowed them to frame it as part of an ongoing ludic tradition within Western game design. *Katamari Damacy*, however, was impossible to fit into any existing category; hence, game critics used terms like "quirky" or "Japanese" as discursive shorthand to signify their sense of alienation from the content and intended experience of the text.

To game criticism, Otherness is a malleable tool, enabling the categorization of any element that is not perceived as part of the ludic tradition of the observer as "foreign" or "weird." The disruptive potential that play habits can have on a cultural framework makes these deviations stand out and be prone to different value judgments. In some cases, like that of *Intelligent Qube*, that judgment results in the search for equivalencies with smaller game genres that already appeal to a niche audience. In cases like *Metal Gear Solid 4*, notions of authorship and the theoretical framework of auteur theory help explain any aspect of the title that does not match critical expectations. When none of these discursive strategies are available, as with *Katamari Damacy*, assumptions are made about cultural distance between the writer and the designer. Yet as the *Katamari* franchise grew, later reviews of subsequent titles began to establish a common analytical framework. Over time, the sense of cultural distance was progressively sublimated by the trappings of auteur theory, assigning more authorial intent to the "quirkiness" of the title.

By analyzing the impact of these titles using Pelletier-Gagnon's terminology,[39] it is possible to establish some commonalities between the reaction to these titles and their mukoseki features. Depending on design sensibilities and marketing practices, these final products have been able to "pass" more and less successfully as "odorless" to the American and European audience. At the same time, the lack of an intentionally "odorless" design in games like *Katamari Damacy* can be largely resolved in game criticism by attributing a sense of Otherness to the design ethos behind them that is either explained with auteur theory or through culturally-charged descriptions that rely on a highly exoticized perception of Japanese society.[40] This perception heavily relies on Orientalist notions of the East and the West and has a long tradition in critical analysis of Japanese media.

While taking into account the specificities that lead some Japanese video-games to become "representative" of their national output, it is important to recognize how that distinction process also prompts Anglophone gaming outlets to construct a sense of cultural exceptionalism that separates Japanese media from other examples. Even when this distinction is framed under a purely theoretical framework, it is still reflected and reinforced by promotional tactics like those used by the Agency for Cultural Affairs, which absorbs external evaluations when assessing the strength of the country's contents output. Such a feedback loop inevitably "recenters" international appreciation of Japanese culture through the most profitable channels in such a way that taste preferences expressed by Anglophone and (to a lesser extent) Spanish-speaking players are catered to first and foremost, while ignoring or relegating others to niche status.[41]

Thus, while *gêmu* is indeed useful in describing and categorizing aspects of game design and artistic presentation that may be particular to Japan's media environment, interpretative communities like those surrounding English-language media use those aspects to construct a sense of cultural exceptionalism that elevates some Japanese media above the mainstream currents of the landscape while excluding others, reinforcing a sense of cultural distance between Japanese games according to their "global" or "niche" appeal. This exceptionalism may be useful to Japanese companies and institutions because it imbues their products with cultural prestige and allows them to leverage their presence as a global cultural force, even as that leverage may be compromised by the imperative of catering to as wide an audience as possible.

Conclusions

From Douglas McGray's influential article to Prime Minister Abe Shinzô wearing a Mario hat during the closing ceremonies of the 2016 Summer Olympics,[42] the cultural significance of Japanese *gêmu* has only increased over time, alongside the circulation of Japanese media. Thanks to a rubric of a recognizable set of features, it is possible to find traces of "Japaneseness" in virtually every aspect of modern game design. Many Japanese games today are developed from the beginning with a mukokuseki framework that aims for global circulation, but they still serve a political function as potential representatives of the Japanese "brand."

A new way of defining Otherness and "Japaneseness" emerges from this circulation, which contributes to the continuous objectification of Japan as either a "cool" or "weird" space of consumption, one that Kumiko Sato eloquently described as "a culture that simultaneously progresses and regresses through technology."[43] Otherization is no longer defined by a set of descriptors that prefigure culture and values, but by a progressive homogenization of media that divides content according to its "universal" or "niche" appeal. Over time, video games that deviate from the norm may be eventually normalized into the ludic tradition of the community, but the assignment of cultural differences as rhetorical shorthand betrays a dualistic vision of the medium between "conventional" games and "unconventional" titles, with unconventional ones distanced as much as possible from the discourse on the medium. In this context of massive circulation, "Japaneseness" is automatically associated with alterity and has an effect on the way that certain textual configurations and narrative arrangements get to be identified with a different value system or cultural tradition. Determining which games conform to the ludic tradition of the critics and players and which do not, as well as understanding the way in which these categorization processes come into being, enables assessment of which elements are more likely to be assigned a sense of Otherness than others. That assessment will be helpful to understand the ways in which Japanese titles have managed to adapt to these categorizations and maintain their influence in foreign markets, which is vital to understand the progression of the medium as an artistic field first and to understand Japan's role in it second.

....

Tomás Grau is a PhD researcher of Media and Cultural Studies at the Autonomous University of Barcelona and member of the GREGAL research group. His research is centered on intercultural processes and power dynamics between Japanese, European, and American cultural industries.

....

Notes

1. Namco, *Katamari Damacy* (published by Namco), 2004 (Japanese release).
2. Edge Staff, "How Katamari Became One of the Most Eccentric Games Ever" (July

2015), https://www.gamesradar.com/how-earnest-little-prince-rolled-eccen tric-classic/ (accessed March 25, 2018).

3. Dean Takahashi, *The Xbox 360 Uncloaked: The Real Story Behind Microsoft's Next-Generation Video Game Console* (Arlington, Va.: SpiderWorks LLC, 2006), 15; Daniel Sloan, *Playing to Wiin: Nintendo and the Video Game Industry's Greatest Comeback* (Singapore: John Wiley & Sons, 2011), 175; Tristan Donovan, *Replay: The History of Video Games* (East Sussex: Yellow Ant, 2010), 355.

4. Hanna Wirman, "Sinological-orientalism in Western News Media," in *Games and Culture* 11, no. 3 (2016): 298–315. Sandra Annett, *Anime Fan Communities: Transcultural Flows and Frictions* (New York: Palgrave MacMillan, 2014), 5.

5. Iwabuchi Koichi, *Recentering Globalization: Popular Culture and Japanese Transnationalism* (Durham: Duke University Press, 2002), 52.

6. Douglas McCray, "Japan's Gross National Cool," *Foreign Policy* 130 (2002). See also Michal Daliot-bul, "Japan Brand Strategy: The Taming of 'Cool Japan' and the Challenges of Cultural Planning in a Postmodern Age," in *Social Science Japan Journal* 12, no. 2 (2009): 251.

7. Ueno Toshiya, "Japanimation and Techno-orientalism: Japan as the Sub-Empire of Signs," in *Documentary Box 9* (1997), https://www.yidff.jp/docbox/9/box9-1-e.html (accessed May 14, 2018).

8. Patrick Galbraith, "'The Lolicon Guy:' Some Observations on Researching Unpopular Topic in Japan," in *The End of Cool Japan: Ethical, Legal, and Cultural Challenges to Japanese Popular Culture*, ed. Mark McLelland (New York: Routledge, 2017), 109.

9. Brian Ashcraft, "The 31 Most Important Japanese Games Ever Made" (December 2016), https://kotaku.com/the-31-most-important-japanese-games-ever-made -1782936854 (accessed March 25, 2018). Sam Byford, "Japan used to rule video games, so what happened?" (March 2014), https://www.theverge.com/2014 /3/20/5522320/final-fight-can-japans-gaming-industry-be-saved (accessed March 25, 2018).

10. Martin Robinson, "The Truth about Japan: A Postcard from the Japanese Games Industry" (October 2012), https://www.eurogamer.net/articles/2012-10-10 -tokyo-story-a-postcard-from-the-japanese-games-industry (accessed March 25, 2018). Kath Brice, "Capcom: Japanese Industry Needs to Evolve to Catch Up with West" (May 2010), https://www.gamesindustry.biz/articles/capcom -japanese-industry-needs-to-evolve-to-catch-up-with-west (accessed March 25, 2018).

11. Famitsu, "Do You Like Recent Japanese Games?" (April 2018), https://www .famitsu.com/news/201804/23155562.html (accessed March 25, 2018).

12. Eric Hobsbawn and Terence O. Ranger, *The Invention of Tradition* (Cambridge: The Press Syndicate of the University of Cambridge, 1983), translated by Omar Rodríguez and published as *La invención de la Tradición* (Barcelona: Crítica, 2002), 8.

13. Anne Allison, "The Japan Fad in Global Youth Culture and Millenial Capitalism," in *Mechademia I: Emerging Worlds of Anime and Manga*, ed. Frenchy Lunning (Minneapolis: University of Minnesota Press, 2006), 11–21.

14. Colin Cremin, "The Formal Qualities of the Video Game: An Exploration of Super Mario Galaxy with Gilles Deleuze," in *Games and Culture* 7, no. 1 (2012): 72–86.

15. Pierre de Bourdieu, *La Distinction: Critique sociale du jugement* (Paris: Les Editions de Minuit, 1979), translated by Mª del Carmen Ruiz Elvira and published as *La Distinción: Criterios y bases sociales del gusto* (Madrid: Taurus), 10.

16. Iwabuchi, *Recentering Globalization*, 94.

17. Jérémie Pelletier-Gagnon, *Video Games and Japaneseness: An Analysis of Localization and Circulation of Japanese Video Games in North America* (Master's Thesis, McGill University, Quebec, 2011). Martin Picard, "The Foundation of Geemu: A Brief History of Early Japanese Video Games," *Game Studies* 13, no. 2 (December 2013), http://gamestudies.org/1302/articles/picard. Antonio Loriguillo-López and Victor Navarro-Remesal, "What Makes Gêmu Different: A Look at the Distinctive Design Traits of Japanese Video Games and Their Place in the Japanese Media Mix," *Journal of Games Criticism* 2, no. 1 (January 2015), http://gamescrit icism.org/articles/navarro-remesalloriguillo-lopez-2-1/ (accessed March 25, 2018).

18. Mia Consalvo and Christopher A. Paul, "Welcome to the Discourse of the Real: Constituting the Boundaries of Games and Players," *FDG* (2013): 55–62.

19. Consalvo and Paul, "Welcome to the Discourse," 2.

20. Pelletier-Gagnon, Video Games and Japaneseness, 11.

21. Loriguillo-López and Navarro-Remesal, "What Makes Gêmu Different," 2.

22. Katja Valaskivi and Joahanna Sumiala, "Circulating Social Imaginaries: Theoretical and Methodological Reflections," *European Journal of Cultural Studies* 17, no. 3 (2013): 229–43.

23. ASCII Games, *RPG Tsukuru* (published by Kadokawa Games), 1992–2015 (Japanese release).

24. Epics, *I. Q.* (published by Sony Computer Entertainment), 1997 (Japanese release). Kojima Productions, *Metal Gear Solid 4: Guns of the Patriots* (published by Konami), 2008 (Japanese release).

25. Media Arts Festival, "Excellence Award—I.Q. Intelligent Qube" (1997), http://archive.j-mediaarts.jp/en/festival/1997-digital-art-interactive/works/01di_iq/ (accessed March 25, 2018).

26. Joe Fielder, "Intelligent Qube Review" (November 1997), https://www.game spot.com/reviews/intelligent-qube-review/1900-2545976/ (accessed March 25, 2018).

27. Squaresoft, *Final Fantasy VII* (published by Sony Computer Entertainment), 1997 (Japanese release).

28. James Mielke, "I.Q. Remix+: Intelligent Qube (Import) Review" (April 2000),

https://www.gamespot.com/reviews/iq-remix-intelligent-qube-import-review /1900-2558014/ (accessed March 25, 2018).

29. Sugar & Rockets, *Yarudora Series* (published by Sony Computer Entertainment), 1998–2006 (Japanese release).

30. Jeremy Parish, "Katamari Damacy Review" (September 2004), https://web .archive.org/web/20050213084603/http://www.1up.com/do/reviewPage?cId =3134713&did=1 (accessed March 25, 2018).

31. L. E. Hall, Katamari Damacy (Los Angeles: Boss Fight Books, 2018).

32. Konami Computer Entertainment Japan, *Metal Gear Solid* (published by Konami), 1998 (Japanese release).

33. Simon Parkin, "Hideo Kojima: Metal Gear Questions US Dominance of the World" (July 2014), https://www.theguardian.com/technology/2014/jul/18/ hideo-kojima-interview-metal-gear-solid-phantom-pain (accessed March 25, 2018).

34. "About MGF" (June 2016), http://series3.homestead.com/about.html (accessed March 25, 2018). Lone Dragon, "A Warrior's Hope" (November 2000), https:// www.fanfiction.net/s/115898/1/A-Warrior-s-Hope (accessed March 25, 2018).

35. Oli Welsh, "Metal Gear Solid 4: Guns of the Patriots Review" (August 2008), http://www.eurogamer.net/articles/metal-gear-solid-4-guns-of-the-patriots -review (accessed March 25, 2018). Konami Computer Entertainment Japan, *Metal Gear Solid 3* (published by Konami Corporation), 2004 (Japanese release).

36. Ubisoft Shanghai and Ubisoft Milan, *Tom Clancy's Splinter Cell: Pandora Tomorrow* (published by Ubisoft), 2004 (North American release).

37. Media Arts Festival, "Excellence Award—Metal Gear Solid 4: Guns of the Patriots" (2007), http://archive.j-mediaarts.jp/en/festival/2007/entertainment/ works/11e_metal_gear_solid_4_guns_of_the_patriots/ (accessed March 25, 2018).

38. Consalvo and Paul, "Discourse of the Real," 3–4.

39. Pelletier-Gagnon, "Video Games and Japaneseness," 16–28.

40. GameCentral, "Understanding the Culture of Japanese Games—Reader's Feature" (April 2013), https://metro.co.uk/2013/04/07/understanding-the-culture -of-japanese-games-readers-feature-3585926/ (accessed March 25, 2018).

41. Alisa Freedman, "*Death Note,* Student Crimes, and the Power of Universities in the Global Spread of Manga," in *The End of Cool Japan: Ethical, Legal, and Cultural Challenges to Japanese Popular Culture,* ed. Mark McLelland (New York: Routledge, 2017), 47.

42. Chiara Palazzo, "Japanese PM Shinzo Abe Appears in Disguise as Super Mario at Rio Olympics Closing Ceremony" (August 2016), https://www.telegraph.co.uk/ olympics/2016/08/22/shinzo-abe-emerges-from-a-green-pipe-disguised-as -super-mario-du/ (accessed March 25, 2018).

43. Kumiko Sato, "How Information Technology Has (Not) Changed Feminism and Japanism Cyberpunk," *Comparative Literature Studies* 41, no. 3 (2004): 335–55.

Disrupting Centers of Transcultural Materialities

The Transnationalization of Japan Cool through Philippine Fan Works

KRISTINE MICHELLE L. SANTOS

In an increasingly networked world, fans of anime and manga converge in online spaces that are often privileged by algorithms of search engines or trending social media platforms. More often than not, these fan spaces simulate a "homogenous" world where fans' geopolitical affiliations disappear in Anglophone discussions of anime and manga. If anything, Japan emerges as a dominant national figure in discussions primarily conducted in English. This is the shape of global Anglophone fandom surrounding anime and manga, where fans from all over the globe converge in online spaces to learn more about the literacies and practices surrounding Japanese popular culture.

Since the popularization of Japanese popular culture in the Philippines in the late 1990s, Filipino fans have actively engaged in these online transcultural spaces. With English as the second official language of the country, Filipino fans who have command of English have easily navigated these online anime and manga communities. Fan practices such as writing fan fiction became opportunities to engage with transcultural online communities and even strengthen their English language skills.[1] Looking at fan spaces such as Fanfiction.net and Archiveofourown.org, expressions of nationality have been limited to a few hundreds of fans and in specific fandoms. The rest of Filipino anime and manga fans are quite content with assimilating into fandom's transcultural space—until recently.

Since 2010, Filipino fans have actively produced fan works that challenge the "homogeneity" of online anime and manga fandom. While the study of localized transcultural materials is not new, my focus in this essay is on the process whereby transcultural fandom becomes a critical space for Filipino fans to learn and develop the literacies that gave them the creative agency to express their nationality in this supposedly "homogenous" space through their fan works.[2] I examine different fan practices and their products, such as the increased Filipino interest in the anthropomorphosis (*gijinka*) of Filipino institutions and local fan attempts to situate the Philippines in the imagination of transcultural fans through *Yuri!!! on Ice* fan works. I argue that fans' local iterations of these transcultural practices challenge the perceived homogeneity of Anglophone fandom while encouraging this transcultural space to embrace and acknowledge diverse multicultural expressions. In the process, I argue that these actions disrupt notions of transcultural homogeneity in these English-language fan spaces, as these transnational materials challenge and dislocate centers of anime and manga fandom.

"Homogeneity" in Transcultural Media and its Fandom

Studies surrounding the globalization of Japanese popular culture have focused on its transnational flows between Japan and other nations in the Americas, Europe, and East Asia.[3] More often than not, transnational analysis of Japanese popular culture focuses on bilateral engagements that highlight the political, cultural, and social intricacies surrounding Japan's attempt at "soft power." Koichi Iwabuchi has argued that Japan's increased efforts to disseminate its brand of nationalism highlight the country's postwar Orientalist strategy.[4] Japan's notion of pop-culture diplomacy has been highly unilateral, as some of its partner countries leave little or no impact on Japanese culture.[5] If anything, the countries that have a kind of impact on Japanese popular culture are those that trigger the Japanese Occidentalist imagination—from England's Victorian aesthetic to Germany's bildungsroman.[6] Rather than building cross-cultural exchanges, Iwabuchi notes that Japan's transcultural engagement seeks to control the consumption of Japanese culture by essentializing its national brand. This engagement diverts consumers' attention from the diversity within Japanese culture that challenges the state's framework.[7] Iwabuchi warns us of how Japan uses its cultural media to create a "homogenous" notion of Japan in a transcultural or trans/national space.[8]

While Iwabuchi highlights the power of the state in shaping a "homogenous" notion of a national culture, Lori Morimoto and Bertha Chin highlight how "affinities of affect" facilitate "homogeneity" as global fans may share affective ties when they consume transcultural media.[9] Affect, as Brian Massumi describes, is an intensity that leads to a visceral response that does not follow logic or consciousness.[10] One can think of an affective response as the involuntary scream a fan makes upon seeing their object of affection, such as their character from their favorite anime or manga. Fans who immerse in transnational media and actively engage with global fan discourse are not connected by their geopolitical proximities but rather by their affective media experiences. As Morimoto and Chin argue, "this concept frees fandom from the constraints of national belonging, reinforcing our contention that fans become fans of border-crossing texts or objects not necessarily because of *where* they are produced, but because they may recognize a subjective moment of affinity regardless of origin."[11]

Morimoto and Chin's notion of transcultural fandom perpetuates the borderlessness of global fandom. To a certain extent, their argument reinforces the idea of Japanese popular media as stateless (*mukokuseki*), whereby anime and manga feature characters and environments divorced from Japanese reality.[12] Since fans are connected via their affective responses to media, geopolitical connections are overlooked, if not forgotten. Affinities of affect highlight the growth of what Henry Jenkins describes as pop cosmopolitanism: "the ways that the transcultural flows of popular inspire new forms of global consciousness and cultural competency."[13] The statelessness of Japanese media and its fandom showcases the potential statelessness of its cultural competencies. For Iwabuchi, this is problematic because at times the term *mukokuseki* implies the erasure of cultural specificities not just of its media but also its audience.[14] While these characteristics of transcultural media and fandom lead to notions of "homogeneity," there are undeniable cultural centers in this space—Japan, the home of the creators and primary audience of this transcultural medium, and the United States, which has a strong influence on the English-language distribution of anime and manga and its fan discourse.

Centers of Transcultural Fan Literacies and Practices: The Case of Japan and America

While it is possible that transnational Japanese popular media facilitate stateless affinities of affect among fans, it is undeniable that fans are also aware of the different transnational dimensions involved in anime and manga fandom. This section examines the different literacies and practices that situate Japan and America as cultural centers in this supposedly "stateless" fan space. The examination of these culturally nuanced literacies, practices, and materials in transcultural fandom highlights how foreign fans who live outside of these countries must acquire these literacies and practices in order to engage in this space. It is important to examine Japanese and American fan literacies and practices that serve as cornerstones for transcultural fandom, for they play a vital role in shaping the fan community overall.

At their core, many literacies and practices in transcultural fandom come from Japanese anime and manga fan culture. Navigating Japan's cultural contents entails knowledge of Japan's complex media landscape, which requires literacies surrounding their various contents and media mixes, their diverse genres, and even their deeply gendered targets—from the brave adventures of shônen stories to the innocence of shôjo romances. Japanese fans also have the literacies to process and dissect these contents into narrative (or non-narrative) elements and concepts that they conceptually store in what Hiroki Azuma describes as a "database."[15] These narrative (or non-narrative) elements comprise visual characteristics, character tropes, settings, themes, and other textual elements that fans organize and intertextually weave in their database. The structure of fans' database can be seen in the ways Japanese fans categorize these elements through their fan works. For example, the different tags or keywords fans use online—from descriptive visual traits such as stray hair (*ahoge*, literally an idiot hair) to relationship tropes such as childhood friends (*osananajimi*)—contribute to fans' database of various narrative or non-narrative elements they have in encountered not just in anime and manga but also in other popular media.

The most notable of these narrative elements elicit an affective response called *moe*, a Japanese word that means either "to sprout" or "to burn." Moe serves as an indication of fans' passion for specific narrative or non-narrative elements. Moe frequently pushes Japanese fans to engage in diverse fan practices, from fervent discussions that reimagine different characters and scenarios to the production of independently published derivative fan magazines (*nijisôsaku dôjinshi*) that contain essays or comics featuring moe elements from their favorite works.[16] These moe elements range from characters, scenarios, and even the relationships between different characters.[17]

One of the more interesting materials emerging from moe is gijinka, anthropomorphic illustrations of various nonliving items, ranging from tanks to nations. The production of these moe gijinka rely on a fans' ability to recognize, process, and produce *kyaramoe*, characters without an original narrative that embody various narrative or design elements that elicit moe.[18] Kyara have been associated with iconic brand mascots such as Hello Kitty or city mascots known as *yurukyara* (wobbly characters) such as Kumamon.[19] But since the late 1970s, Japanese fans have also reimagined characters and even non-existent items as kyara, often inspired by various narrative experimentation in manga. Fans' reimagined kyara have appeared in fan works, such as illustrations and dôjinshi, which in turn serve as media for affective hermeneutics.

Anne Wilson describes affective hermeneutics as "a set way of gaining knowledge through feelings," whereby fans can use fan works to "direct focus towards moments of high emotion in a text to stimulate equally strong feelings in the reader; these heighten a sense of empathy, connection, or intimacy between the readers and the character in the text."[20] While Wilson analyzed English-language fan fiction, the same can be said of fan works such as dôjinshi that fans use to provoke affective responses from their readers. Fan works such as moe gijinka elicit affect from readers through the personification of items and concepts. Since the early 2000s, fans have shared imagined lives of tanks, swords, and even nations.

One of the more successful moe gijinka works is *Hetalia: Axis Powers* (2006), a webcomic featuring the complex relationship between the nations involved in World War II. In seeing the handsome straight-laced Germany protect the adorably clumsy Italy while fighting against the regally arrogant England and the courageous America, *Hetalia* fans are able to understand and learn the different stereotypes used to personify these nations.[21] The webcomic became a success and was eventually distributed in mainstream Japanese media. *Hetalia* became a global phenomenon, highlighting the transcultural power of affective narratives.[22] Japanese popular media such as *Hetalia* not only taught foreign fans creative concepts such as moe gijinka but also served as gateways to fan practices associated with anime and manga fan culture such as coupling (*kappuringu*), in which characters, whether homoerotic or not, are imagined sharing intimate relationships.[23] Associated with coupling are fan products such as fan dôjinshi, where the diverse potential of kyara are explored as they are embedded in new situations, relationships, and narratives. Japanese fans' playful reimagining of different narrative elements from their databases leads to texts that elicit visceral responses via new combinations of narrative and visual elements. The more foreign fans affectively react to anime and manga fan dôjinshi, the more they learn about the different literacies embedded in the media and the practices emerging from its consumption.

Engaging with Japanese fandom, however, requires not only language literacies but also competency in regards to their nuanced literacies and practices. Foreign fans who understand Japanese have the advantage of building their cultural competencies without language acting as a hurdle. Early foreign enthusiasts like Frederik Schodt and Rachel Matt Thorn played a critical role in translating various aspects of Japan's complex popular culture for an audience whose language happens to be the most widely used language in the world: English.

It is important to recognize that America is the center of Anglophone anime and manga products and transcultural fan literacies. United States-based companies such as Viz and Crunchyroll have a hand in the distribution of English-language anime and manga all over the globe. Many of these companies have capitalized on the enthusiasm of fans who were more than eager to contribute to the distribution of these anime and manga in the English-language community. More often than not, fervent American fans of anime and manga contribute to these companies, which have control over translated Japanese pop culture news and media. Sites such as Crunchyroll regularly translate news and media from Japan and have become a rich resource of information and opinion in Anglophone fandom. Fans who write for these Anglophone anime and manga sites become "Big Name Fans," although it is important to note that other Japanese-literate Anglophone fans who are active on social media platforms, such as Twitter and Tumblr, have also influenced transcultural anime and manga fandom through their quick dissemination of information, especially when they report news on specific fan events in Japan.

Within the Anglophone transcultural anime and manga fandom are sets of literacies and practices that are just as elaborate and extensive as Japanese fans' intertextual database. Henry Jenkins describes transcultural fan knowledge as "encyclopaedic" and it too serves as a rich resource for various fan products such as fan translations, fanfiction and fanart.[24] Specific to anime and manga fandom are various Japanese words that are employed by transcultural fandom in an effort to retain the authenticity of various cultural concepts and to develop the cultural competencies of foreign fans. When fan translations dominated Anglophone transcultural fandom in the early 2000s, some fan groups made clear efforts to retain critical Japanese fan jargon, which they explained with extensive notes littering the margins of manga pages or anime frames. Their practices shaped the English localization of anime and manga as fans sought authenticity in legally distributed Japanese media.[25] American anime and manga publishers and distributors continued some of these practices while educating fans about the process of translation and localization. It is important to note that many of these English-language localizers are American companies targeting the North American market. As such, many of their decisions are influenced by the literacies and practices of American fans. Additionally, many English-language bookstores all over the globe stock the American releases of Japanese manga.

Beyond the cultural nuances maintained in commercial Anglophone media, fanfiction is just as effective as dôjinshi in facilitating affective affinity, for it too is a central tool for affective hermeneutics. Fanfiction is often the entry point for foreign anime and manga enthusiasts into transcultural fandom. More than dôjinshi, English-speaking fans tend to discover various fan communities where discussions surrounding their favorite series are embedded in reimagined fictional narratives. Much like dôjinshi, fanfiction also has its own lexicon (such as *omegaverse*) that fans learn as part of the process of being affected by the text. Over the years, as fanfiction archives became increasingly complex, writers and readers began to learn fandom's lexicon through the different keywords and tags used to describe these texts. Archiveofourown.org, one of the largest repositories of English fan fiction online, also uses elaborate tags and categories that clearly categorize fanfic content, which helps build readers' expectations.

Even fan scanlation aggregator sites use their own keywords to categorize Japanese manga by genre, themes, and narrative elements. The categorization used by these English-language fan sites functions as an informative index of translated Japanese knowledge, which in turn shapes readers' knowledge of Japanese media. At times, these categories are problematic as they may misinform fans. For example, Japanese Boys' Love (BL) titles in English-language manga aggregator sites are often described as *yaoi* or *shonen'ai*. In Japan, "BL" refers to a commercial manga genre featuring original romances between two men, while "shonen'ai" refers to early homoerotic romances in shojo manga during the 1970s, and "yaoi" is highly associated with homoerotic fan dôjinshi prominent in the 1980s and 1990s. On English-language fan sites, yaoi is taken out of its Japanese fan context and used to describe any commercial BL manga with sexual scenes, while shonen'ai is also divorced from BL manga history, as it is used to describe commercial BL titles without sexual scenes. The misuse of keywords to describe genre and narrative elements in manga impacts readers who immediately learn associations by virtue of their affective experiences. These kinds of mislabeling have in some cases even caused fissures between Japanese and Anglophone fan cultures.

Beyond the English-translated knowledge produced in transcultural fandom, American fans also have a strong influence on the kinds of *products* that fans produce. As early as 2013, on sites such as Tumblr, not only did

American fan illustrators share their works online but they also began to actively market the sale of their illustrations as postcards, stickers, and eventually, acrylic keychains and stands. Most of these artists would sell these fan products at American fan events such as Anime Expo. While postcards and posters were not new, the sale of stickers and accessories became increasingly common and is now the majority of fan materials sold at American fan events.

Another American product that diverges from Japanese practices is the production and sale of illustration fanzines. Unlike contemporary dôjinshi, which mostly consist of comic content and are produced by individual creators, fanzines popularized by American artists are highly collaborative and primarily features illustrations following a theme. The process often begins on sites like Tumblr with a call for participation by a fanzine editor, who is then responsible for collating submissions and printing the work. The result is closer to a colored illustration book. Some artists also self-publish their own illustration fanzines. While it is generally accepted that fanzines are synonymous with dôjinshi, it is important to note that Anglophone anime and manga fans have not used the term *dôjinshi* to refer to their fanzines. It is unclear whether this decision is due to concerns regarding cultural appropriation but it is important to note that creators of fanzines are conscious of the differences between these two types of zines.

The influence of these two transcultural fan centers, Japan and America, can be widely seen in the variety of materials created and sold in fan events around Australia and Southeast Asia, as well as online spaces such as Facebook and Instagram. The literacies and practices of Japan and America thus also have an impact on the kinds of fan materials produced by Filipinos.

Transcultural Fandom and Japanese Popular Culture in Filipino Fandom

Understanding where Filipino fans situate themselves within this transcultural fandom demands an examination of the Philippines as a captive market for anime and manga and Filipino fans' access to and engagement with online spaces. Knowing the transnational flows of anime and manga materials into the Philippines contributes to the understanding of markets and audiences that operate outside transcultural centers like Japan and North America.

The 2014 Cool Japan presentation released by the Japanese Ministry of Economy, Trade, and Industry (METI) identified the Philippines as a potential market for Japanese fashion.[26] Unlike other countries in Southeast Asia such as Indonesia, Singapore and Thailand, Japan does not see the Philippines as a cultural hub for its contents industry despite it being the base of one of the largest animation studios in Japan, Toei Animation. This perception is primarily informed by Filipino audiences displaying fervent interest in and active engagement with Japanese contents for a decade yet failing to become a captive market for these goods.

Philippine anime fandom existed as early as the late 1970s when Japanese robot animation such as *Chôdenji mashîn borutesu V* (Super electromagnetic machine voltes five, 1977-78) and *Mazinger Z* (1972-73) captivated the hearts of young viewers before they were actively banned by the Marcos regime after parents complained that these Japanese shows were too violent for children.[27] By the 1980s and early 1990s, shows such *Robotech* (1985), *Candy Candy* (1976-79), and *Sekai meisaku gekijô* (*World Masterpiece Theatre*, 1969-2009) were shown on television but were disassociated with Japan. It was only in 1998, when television stations reintroduced some of the earlier banned shows on television, that Japan was again associated with animated works. For a good decade, Philippine media actively bought Japanese animation and regularly showed it as part of after-school television.

The rising popularity of anime on local TV also coincided with the growth of internet culture in the Philippines. This meant that, for some tech-savvy fans, getting access to anime entailed knowing which online communities to tap into to order the latest fan-subbed VHS tapes. While there were limited official English-language anime available, only upper-middle class Filipinos could afford these items. In addition to these, Filipino-Chinese imported pirated anime videos from Hong Kong and Taiwan. Even migrant workers in Japan brought home untranslated secondhand anime or recorded videos. As such, early anime videos distributed in the Philippines were primarily pirated material. Even with the recent surge of specialized cable channels showing anime around the clock, pirates still have quicker access to new anime, while anime on mainstream television has been slowly replaced by Korean television dramas after interests in broadcasted anime started to fade in 2010.

As for manga, some of the earliest available manga in the Philippines were Chinese-translated copies available in Manila's Chinatown. Migrant workers from Japan also tried to bring secondhand manga into the Philippines, but these shops closed after the anime boom ended. However, most Filipinos do not have the proficiency in Japanese. From 2011 to 2017, around 46,000 Filipinos have passed the Japanese Language Proficiency Exam.[28] With English as one of the official state languages, Filipinos have better opportunities to consume English-translated manga. Local comic shops and bookstores have tried to bring in English-translated manga, but these imported comics are quite expensive for an average Filipino.[29]

In 2003, a large local publisher, Summit Media, attempted to produce reprints of *Slam Dunk* (1990–96) under the English-language license of Singaporean comic publisher Chuang Yi. The prices of these editions were reasonable yet their production was discontinued within a few years. In 2009, J-Line Comics became the first publisher to license and distribute manga, namely *Doraemon* (1969–96) and *Detective Conan* (1994–present, *Meitantei Conan*), in Filipino, selling manga volumes at prices that were accessible to young readers but at newsprint quality. One of the larger publishers in the Philippines, PSICOM, attempted to bring in popular titles such as *Fairy Tail* (2006–17) and *Attack on Titan* (2009–present, *Shingeki no kyôjin*) in 2015, but these too were discontinued. Of the many publishers that attempted to bring manga to the Philippines, only J-Line survived with two titles under its belt. Given that the Philippines heavily imports English-language books, it is interesting to note that local manga is far from being commercially mainstream.[30] On the shelves of Manila bookstores, manga are hardly stocked compared to graphic novels from American comic publishers, leading American manga publishers to consider the Philippines an unreliable gray market. The Filipino comic community also has its reservations about manga, especially when it competes with local artistry.[31]

Given the failures of commercial anime and manga in the Philippines, Japan's decision to recalibrate its trade with the Philippines to focus on things other than Japanese contents is appropriate. As a market, Filipinos are not buying official goods, despite the growth of fandom surrounding anime and manga. One of the country's largest anime and manga events, Cosplay Mania, hosted 38,000 attendees in 2017 for two days.[32] Cosplay Mania has also managed to invite renowned Japanese creators and artists for their events. The large fan base at this event highlights how Filipino fans continue to access anime and manga albeit through nonconventional means.

An indication of where Filipino fans may access Japanese popular contents can be seen through the amount of time Filipinos spend online. According to "We Are Social's 2018 Digital in Southeast Asia" report, Filipinos spend around nine hours and twenty-nine minutes online per day, three hours of which are spent watching videos.[33] While the report did not indicate any specific anime streaming sites, some of the most frequented sites by Filipinos are streaming sites for pirated media.[34] Filipinos are also heavy users of Facebook; in terms of their engagement with social media platforms used by fans, only Twitter and Pinterest registers as similarly frequented sites.[35] This implies that popular fan spaces such as Tumblr have less influence compared to these three social media platforms.

The disproportion of Filipinos' access, consumption, and engagement with Japanese popular culture and transcultural fandom may be an indication of social, political, economic, and technological barriers that prevent fair transnational exchange. This leads one to question the influence of transcultural centers such as Japan and America on Filipino fan practices and the materials they produce.

Sexy Sexy Universities and the Filipinization of Gijinka

While mascots have been a part of Filipino branding and culture, the idea of the mascot as a kyara was not part of the imagination of Filipinos until 2012, when a student started to imagine the potential of creating characters that personified some of the major universities in the Philippines. Initially called *Sexy Sexy Universities* on Tumblr, the student's concept eventually inspired a community on Facebook called *Buhay Kolehiyo (BuKo)*, which has over 27,000 members.[36]

On *BuKo*'s Facebook page, the moderators laid the foundation of the *Buhay Kolehiyo* universe by outlining the different visual and personality profiles of these universities.[37] These notes are similar to the character books often associated with popular Japanese series and these serve as a database that can be useful for fans who wish to reproduce these characters in their own fan works.[38] Moderators of the community also produce fan comics, which are critical in building readers' affective attachments to the characters. By virtue of reading the comics, readers are able to view the different universities as kyara: the personification of De La Salle University endlessly flirts with his rival, Neo, the personification of Ateneo de Manila University (Figure 1).

Beyond the comics and the illustrations shared on the website, the kyara of these universities are also produced as keychains and stickers. Only the moderators of the community produce materials for this fandom and fans are discouraged to produce their own. Whether this action is a precautionary measure against potential lawsuits or an action that shows the moderators' desire to have full economic control of the text is unclear. What is clear is

Figure 1. A screenshot of a *Buhay Kolehiyo* comic posted on Facebook and the affective responses of its readers. On the left, Neo claims to have stolen Salle's clothes and reprimands Salle for being flirtatious. On the right, fans react to the image.

that by adapting kyara literacies and using it to reimagine universities in the same way that *Hetalia* has reimagined Axis nations, *Buhay Kolehiyo* produces materials specific to the imagination of young Filipino students and thus, showcases fan practices that are no longer associated with Japan and materials that have no market in Japan or even America.

Philippine Fan Materials in the Transcultural Imagination of *Yuri!!! on Ice*

In the last quarter of 2016, fans all over the globe anticipated the collaboration between director Sayo Yamamoto and manga artist Mitsurou Kubo on a figure skating anime titled *Yuri!!! on Ice (YOI)*. Anime enthusiasts were already excited to see a new sports anime, but the first episode also showcased the series' potential as a queer text. The queer potential of *YOI* was openly welcomed by the Anglophone transcultural fandom. Given that transcultural fans were also engaged with queer fan works, *YOI*'s openness to queer interpretation made it a safe space, especially when the sport of figure skating itself does not appear to be very supportive of its queer athletes.[39] It also helped that figure skating personalities such as Johnny Weir acknowledged the series as a positive example of athleticism and sportsmanship.[40]

What distinguishes *Yuri!!! on Ice* as a transnational work is that its characters operate in a highly global setting. The main character, Yuri Katsuki, is a world-class skater who competes in global competitions. As he travels from one city to another for his competitions, audiences are taken to new places where, like the main character, they learn a bit of local culture. Yuri encounters athletes from Russia to Thailand and he develops healthy relationships with his rivals. The series simulates transcultural fandom as Yuri easily builds connections with figure skaters all over the globe. While the series gives the impression that these figure skaters lose their sense of nation as they focus on their sport and relationships, fans in the Philippines saw this as an acknowledgment of their Southeast Asian identity, especially with the presence of the Thai character, Pichit Chulanont.

For Filipino fans of *Yuri!!! on Ice*, Phichit Chulanont represented the Filipino Olympic skater Michael Christian Martinez, who was the first Southeast Asian figure skater in the winter Olympics. It is unclear as to why Kubo and Yamamoto chose Thailand to represent Southeast Asian skaters, but Filipino fans appreciated the recognition. The series itself was so well-loved by the community that even before the series ended, a group of fervent Filipino fans announced the first *YOI*-only event in Southeast Asia, YOICONPH.[41] The creation of YOICONPH follows the pattern set by specialized fan events dedicated to only one series in Japan. YOICONPH inspired other fans in Southeast Asia to host their own *YOI* events as well.[42]

Not only did *Yuri!!! on Ice* events inspired fans to create a space to celebrate the series, they also inspired creators to produce various fan works for the series. The materials fans produced for fan events such as YOICONPH ranged from transcultural fandom favorites such stickers, postcards, and posters to acrylic stands and enamel pins. However, some of these fanworks were heavily localized, as though the characters of *Yuri!!! on Ice* were intimately familiar with Filipino culture and practices. This entailed the production of fan goods such as stickers, portraying *YOI* characters working part-time in local fast food chains or dressing in *barong*, a local dress-shirt for men. Some fans imagined *YOI* characters as students at Philippine universities. The different materials produced by Filipino fans of *YOI* highlight fans' desire to situate the series within a local context. These products highlight Filipino fans' localized engagement with the series and a market who also appreciates these localized materials. These products also showcase fans' desire to see *YOI* engage with Philippine culture in the same way the series has shown its characters immerse in various cultures. The Philippine localization of *YOI* becomes apparent in the various merchandise lists they share on their social media accounts. In the process, transcultural fandom becomes aware of Filipino culture.

One of the best examples of this phenomenon is *Tara Na!* (*Let's Go!*), a fanzine that gathered Filipino artists to create a travel album where the characters of *Yuri!!! on Ice* visit major sites from all the provinces of the Philippines (Figure 2). The zine comes with various additional merchandise, sowing the characters as either eating local snacks or riding a *jeepney*, a local means of transportation. The editors dedicated the zine to the community, artists, and even the Philippines itself, hoping that "this zine encourages everyone to know more about the stories behind your [the Philippines] marvelous lands and oceans."[43] The zine is also dedicated to the creators of the series as they gave the fan artists "the chance to share our love for our country."[44] Beyond the local sights the artists drew, they also included descriptions that gave readers a sense of local, if not regional, culture. Just as fascinating is the editors' choice to use English as the language of the zine. The fanzine highlights the desire of Filipino fans to invite transcultural fandom to engage with Philippine fandom and culture. The zine also seeks to broaden transcultural imagination by featuring various sights in the Philippines.

The *Tara Na!* zine highlights the growth of fanzine culture in the Philippines. While the Philippines has a rich zine culture, fanzines only to appear in anime and manga fan spaces in 2006. By 2018, at spaces like YOICONPH, more than a third of attendees produced fanzines, some of which were inspired by comic *dôjinshi*. One Filipino artist, Tanaw, has been actively producing illustration and comics for *Yuri!!! on Ice* (Figure 3). Since 2017, Tanaw has actively participated at various *YOI* events in Japan and Southeast Asia. That same year, Japanese *dôjin* company Toranoana contacted her to translate and distribute one of her fanzines for all Toranoana branches.[45] Tanaw's presence in Japan, alongside other Southeast Asians who are also selling their works in Japan, highlights an interesting turn wherein Southeast Asians are now being accommodated in Japanese fan spaces.

One hurdle artists like Tanaw face is language. Tanaw has to produce Japanese-language editions of her *dôjinshi*. At the same time, Tanaw also has to adjust her comics in such a way that they are easier for Japanese readers to read. Her recently published *dôjinshi*, *Afterglow* and *Dance with Me*, follow the

Figure 2. The *Tara Na!* fanzine (upper right) and its different merchandise (clockwise) which include stickers featuring characters eating Philippine snacks, a pouch with an illustration of the characters on a Philippine plane, a notepad featuring a local game that involves climbing a bamboo pole, acrylic keychains, and a postcard featuring a jeepney, a local mode of transportation. Photograph by the author.

reading direction seen in manga, in which texts and images flow from right to left. This pattern differs from most fanzines produced in America and the Philippines, in which comics are read from left to right. To a certain extent, because of the different literacies involved with manga and Western comics, Philippine comic fanzines do not have a single standard, which can be con-

Figure 3. A spread of Tanaw's *Yuri!!! on Ice* fanzines. The image on the upper right features Tanaw's fanzine distributed at Toranoana. Notice how her work maintains English onomatopoeia for the sound effects. Photograph by the author.

fusing for readers trying to adapt to variable reading practices. Nonetheless, the presence of artists like Tanaw highlights the increasing agency of Filipino fans wishing to be recognized as active contributors to transcultural fandom, whether in Japan or in Anglophone spaces.

Disrupting the "Homogeneity" of Transcultural Centers

These Filipino fan products are examples of highly localized materials circulating in anime and manga's transcultural community. Since YOICONPH, some Filipino fans have even placed icons of Philippine flags beside their

Twitter handles to showcase their desire to express their culture in transcultural spaces. For years, many Filipino fans learned the various literacies and practices from transcultural centers such as Japan and America in order to engage with global anime and manga fandom. Many of these fans have learned to produce similar materials as those produced by American and Japanese fans, but in recent years, Filipino fans have chosen to use these literacies to express their own culture. A new sense of pride emanates from many Filipino fans when transcultural fandom recognizes and respects these expressions of diverse identity within the fandom.

The materialities produced by Filipino fans also present a move away from the materialities that Japan and America are offering. Local fans are increasingly producing items, from fanzines to acrylic items, that render the materialities of transcultural fandom accessible in the Philippines and around the region. This new consumer cycle surrounding fan works that are emerging in Southeast Asia may not currently be as large as Japan's Comic Market but, given its rapid growth, it has the potential to become so. For importers of manga and content producers in Japan, this fan market in the Philippines represents another hurdle for the growth of their legal commerce in the country: there is good money circulating around the production of these fan works. Since 2016, craft shops in Manila have capitalized on this fan industry by selling these fan goods in various shops all over the city. The proliferation of fan works in these shops showcases the growth of an economy that seizes opportunities to capitalize on Filipino fans' affective labor and consumption. In the process, consumption of anime and manga centers not on legal commerce but on fan works, further decentralizing Japan and America.

The growth of the Filipino anime and manga fan economy highlights the transnationalization of Japan's transnational cool. The dependency of Filipino fans on the local fan economy challenges the influence of both Japan and the United States in anime and manga production and fandom. Their highly localized fan works challenge the "homogeneity" of anime and manga fandom, which was seen as stateless. At the same time, the production of localized materials taps specific affective affinities. Foreigners who wish to engage with these Filipino fan materialities must now develop their literacies for Filipino culture. As seen in products such as *Tara Na!*, Filipino fans are more than happy to share their culture to global fandom. The presence of Filipino fan creators in Japan and all over Southeast Asia symbolizes the region's enthusiasm in embracing these works. It is now a question of whether Filipino fan materialities will grow in a global fan climate that polices the authenticities of cultural materialities, and how they will relate to industries that seek to control or to capitalize on their affective labors

....

Kristine Michelle L. Santos is Assistant Professor in the Department of History and Japanese Studies Program teaching gender, media, and Asian history at the Ateneo de Manila University, Philippines. Her research interests include Asian youth media history and culture, production of women's new media literacies and practices, and the transnationalization of global popular culture in Asia. Santos has published articles on popular culture in Asia in *The End of Cool Japan* (Routledge 2016; with Febriani Sihombing) and in *Global Manga: "Japanese" Comics Without Japan* (Bloomsbury 2015; with Karl Cheng Chua).

....

Notes

1. Rebecca W. Black, "Online Fan Fiction, Global Identities, and Imagination," *Research in the Teaching of English* 43, no. 4 (2009): 397–425.
2. Rayna Denison, "Transcultural Creativity in Anime: Hybrid Identities in the Production, Distribution, Texts and Fandom of Japanese Anime," *Creative Industries Journal* 3, no. 3 (January 2011): 221–35, https://doi.org/10.1386/cij.3.3.221_1; Charlie Yi Zhang, "When Feminist Falls in Love with Queer: Dan Mei Culture as a Transnational Apparatus of Love," *Feminist Formations* 29, no. 2 (2017): 121, https://doi.org/10.1353/ff.2017.0019.
3. Hye-Kyung Lee, "Participatory Media Fandom: A Case Study of Anime Fansubbing," *Media, Culture & Society* 33, no. 8 (November 22, 2011): 1131–47, https://doi.org/10.1177/0163443711418271; Andrea Wood, "Boys' Love Anime and Queer Desires in Convergence Culture: Transnational Fandom, Censorship and Resistance," *Journal of Graphic Novels and Comics* 4, no. 1 (June 1, 2013): 44–63; Casey Brienza, *Manga in America: Transnational Book Publishing and the Domestication of Japanese Comics* (London: Bloomsbury Academic, 2016); Matt Hills, "Transnational Cult and/as Neoliberalism: The Liminal Economies of Anime Fansubbers," *Transnational Cinemas* 8, no. 1 (February 2017): 80–94, https://doi.org/10.1080/20403526.2016.1245921; Paul Malone, "The Manga Publishing Scene in Europe," in *Manga: An Anthology of Global and Cultural Perspectives*, ed. Toni Johnson-Woods (New York: Continuum Books, 2010), 315–31; Björn-Ole Kamm, "Rotten Use Patterns: What Entertainment Theories Can Do for the Study of Boys' Love," *Transformative Works and Cultures*, no. 12 (2013), http://journal.transformativeworks.org/index.php/twc/article/view/427; Nicole Lamerichs, "Euromanga: Hybrid Styles and Stories in Transcultural Manga Production," in *Global Manga: Japanese Comics without Japan?*, ed. Casey Brienza (Farnham:

Ashgate, 2015), 75–94; Antonija Cavcic, "Sporting the Gothic Look: Refashioning the Gothic Mode in German Manga Trends," in *Global Manga*, 147–66; Liu Ting, "Conflicting Discourses on Boys Love and Subcultural Tactics in Mainland China and Hong Kong," *Intersections: Gender and Sexuality in Asia and the Pacific*, no. 20 (April 2009), http://intersections.anu.edu.au/issue20/liu.htm; Asako P Saito, "Moe and Internet Memes: The Resistance and Accommodation of Japanese Popular Culture in China," *Cultural Studies Review*, no. 1 (2017): 136; Jin-Shiow Chen, "Beautiful, Meaning and Powerful: Explorations of the Bishojo (Beautiful Girl)" and "'Bishonen (Beautiful Boy)' in Taiwan's Anime/Manga Fan Culture," in *International Perspectives on Shojo and Shojo Manga: The Influence of Girl Culture*, ed. Masami Toku (London: Routledge, 2015), 109–19; Ling Yang, "The World of Grand Union: Engendering Trans/Nationalism via Boys' Love in Chinese Online Hetalia Fandom," in *Boys' Love, Cosplay, and Androgynous Idols: Queer Fan Cultures in Mainland China, Hong Kong, and Taiwan*, ed. Maud Lavin, Jing Jamie Zhao, and Ling Yang (Hong Kong: Hong Kong University Press, 2017), 45–62.

4. Koichi Iwabuchi, "Uses of Japanese Popular Culture: Trans/Nationalism and Postcolonial Desire for 'Asia,'" *Emergences: Journal for the Study of Media & Composite Cultures* 11, no. 2 (November 2001): 199–222.

5. Koichi Iwabuchi, "Pop-Culture Diplomacy in Japan: Soft Power, Nation Branding and the Question of 'International Cultural Exchange,'" *International Journal of Cultural Policy* 21, no. 4 (2015): 419–32.

6. Elizabeth Ho, "Victorian Maids and Neo-Victorian Labour in Kaoru Mori's Emma: A Victorian Romance," *Neo-Victorian Studies* 6, no. 2 (September 2013): 40–63; Minori Ishida, *Hisoyaka na kyōiku: Yaoi/bōizu rabu zenshi* (A Secret Education: The prehistory of yaoi/boys' love) (Tokyo: Rakuhoku Shuppan, 2008), 52–57; James Welker, "A Brief History of Shōnen'Ai, Yaoi, and Boys Love," in *Boys' Love Manga and Beyond: History, Culture, and Community in Japan*, ed. Mark McLelland, Kazumi Nagaike, and Katsuhiko Suganuma (Jackson: University Press of Mississippi, 2015), 50; Matt Thorn, "The Moto Hagio Interview in The Comics Journal," Matt-Thorn.Com (blog), July 2005, http://www.mattthorn.com/shoujo_manga/hagio_interview.php.

7. Koichi Iwabuchi, "Undoing Inter-National Fandom in the Age of Brand Nationalism," *Mechademia* 5, no. 1 (November 10, 2010): 92.

8. Iwabuchi, "Uses of Japanese Popular Culture."

9. Bertha Chin and Lori Hitchcock Morimoto, "Towards a Theory of Transcultural Fandom," *Participations* 10, no. 1 (May 2013): 92–108.

10. Brian Massumi, *Parables for the Virtual: Movement, Affect, Sensation* (Durham: Duke University Press Books, 2002), 15–37.

11. Chin and Morimoto, "Towards a Theory of Transcultural Fandom," 99.

12. Susan J. Napier, *Anime from Akira to Princess Mononoke: Experiencing Contemporary Japanese Animation* (New York: Palgrave, 2001), 24–27.

13. Henry Jenkins, "Pop Cosmopolitanism: Mapping Cultural Flows in an Age of Media Convergence," in *Globalization: Culture and Education in the New Millennium*, ed. Marcelo Suárez-orozco and Desirée B. Qin-Hilliard (Berkeley: University of California Press, 2004), 117.

14. Koichi Iwabuchi, *Recentering Globalization: Popular Culture and Japanese Transnationalism* (Durham: Duke University Press Books, 2002), 71.

15. Hiroki Azuma, *Otaku: Japan's Database Animals* (Minneapolis: University of Minnesota Press, 2009).

16. Patrick W. Galbraith, "Moe Talk: Affective Communication among Female Fans of Yaoi in Japan," in *Boys' Love Manga and Beyond*, 153–68.

17. "Otome No Moe o Saguru [Let's Investigate the Otome's Moe]," *Puff*, December 2004.

18. A *kyara* is a truncation of character. For more on *kyara* see Azuma, *Otaku: Database Animals*, 35–53; Hirohito Miyamoto, "How Characters Stand Out," trans. Thomas Lamarre, *Mechademia* 6, no. 1 (2011): 84–91.

19. Kazuhito Isomura, Kazunori Suzuki, and Katsuyuki Tochimoto, "The Evolution of Characters Business Models in Japan: Duffy, Hello Kitty, and Kumamon," *Strategic Direction* 31, no. 4 (2015): 34–37; Christine Yano, Pink Globalization: Hello Kitty's Trek across the Pacific (Durham: Duke University Press Books, 2013); Debra J. Occhi, "Wobbly Aesthetics, Performance, and Message: Comparing Japanese Kyara with Their Anthropomorphic Forebears," *Asian Ethnology*, no. 1 (2012): 109–32.

20. Anna Wilson, "The Role of Affect in Fan Fiction," *Transformative Works and Cultures*, no. 21 (2016), http://journal.transformativeworks.org/index.php/twc/article/view/684.

21. Toshio Miyake, "Doing Occidentalism in Contemporary Japan: Nation Anthropomorphism and Sexualized Parody in Axis Powers Hetalia," *Transformative Works and Cultures*, no. 12 (2013): 4–5, https://doi.org/10.3983/twc.2013.0436.

22. Yang, "The World of Grand Union: Engendering Trans/Nationalism via Boys' Love in Chinese Online Hetalia Fandom."

23. Patrick W. Galbraith, "Moe and the Potential of Fantasy in Post-Millennial Japan," *Electronic Journal of Contemporary Japanese Studies*, October 31, 2009, http://www.japanesestudies.org.uk/articles/2009/Galbraith.html.

24. Henry Jenkins, "Transmedia Storytelling 101," *Henry Jenkins*, March 21, 2007, http://henryjenkins.org/blog/2007/03/transmedia_storytelling_101.html.

25. Cathy Sell, "Manga Translation and Interculture," *Mechademia* 6, no. 1 (2011): 93–108, https://doi.org/10.1353/mec.2011.0002.

26. "Cool Japan Initiative," Cool Japan/Creative Industry Policy-Ministry of Economy, Trade, and Industry (METI), July 2014, 21, http://www.meti.go.jp/policy/mono_info_service/mono/creative/file/1406CoolJapanInitiative.pdf.

27. Herbeth Fondevilla, "Contemplating the Identity of Manga in the Philippines," *International Journal of Comic Art* 9, no. 2 (2007): 445.

28. Japan Foundation, "Previous Test Data," Japanese Language Proficiency Test, https://www.jlpt.jp/statistics/archive.html (accessed June 10, 2018).

29. Philippine Statistics Authority, "2015 Family Income and Expenditure Survey," *Philippine Statistic Authority*, https://psa.gov.ph/content/2015-fies-additional -tables (accessed June 9, 2018).

30. Neni Sta. Romana-Cruz, "State of the Book Industry Address," *National Book Development Board* (blog), May 22, 2014, http://booksphilippines.gov.ph/state -of-the-book-industry-address-2/.

31. Kristine Michelle Santos and Febriani Sihombing, "Is There a Space for Cool Manga in Indonesia and the Philippines? Postcolonial Discourses on Transcultural Manga," in *The End of Cool Japan: Ethical, Legal, and Cultural Challenges to Japanese Popular Culture*, ed. Mark McLelland (London; New York: Routledge, 2016), 196–218.

32. "Cosplay Mania 2018 Sales Kit," 2018, 4.

33. We Are Social, "Digital in 2018 in Southeast Asia," (Internet, 18:15:38 UTC), 111, https://www.slideshare.net/wearesocial/digital-in-2018-in-southeast-asia -part-2-southeast-86866464?from_action=save.

34. We Are Social, 119.

35. We Are Social, 125.

36. "Sexy Sexy Universities," SSU via Tumblr, http://sexysexyuniversities.tumblr .com/ (accessed June 12, 2018); "Buhay Kolehiyo," Buhay Kolehiyo via Facebook, https://www.facebook.com/sexysexyuniversities/ (accessed June 8, 2018).

37. "Buhay Kolehiyo's Visual Guide," Buhay Kolehiyo via Facebook, July 26, 2017, https://www.facebook.com/sexysexyuniversities/photos/a.1875383206030625 .1073741828.1760706184164995/1982403248661953/?type=3&theater; "The Great [Unorganized] Uni Info Document," Buhay Kolehiyo via Facebook, April 20, 2017, https://www.facebook.com/notes/buhay-kolehiyo/the-great-unorga nized-uni-info-document/1928243724077906/.

38. Masashi Kishimoto, *Naruto hiden: Rin no sho kyarakutā ofisharu dēta bukku* [*Naruto secrets: The scroll of challenges*-Character official data book] (Tokyo: Shūeisha, 2002).

39. Palmer Haasch, "'Yuri!!! On Ice' and the Importance of Positive LGBTQ Representation," GLAAD, August 9, 2017, https://www.glaad.org/blog/yuri-ice-and -importance-positive-lgbtq-representation; Eoin O'Callaghan, "Adam Rippon, John Curry and Figure Skating's Complex History with Gay Athletes," *The Guardian*, February 17, 2018, sec. Sport, http://www.theguardian.com/ sport/2018/feb/17/adam-rippon-lgbt-figure-skaters-john-curry.

40. Lauren Orsini, "Catching Up On 'Yuri!!! on Ice' With Figure Skater Johnny Weir," *Forbes*, August 31, 2017, https://www.forbes.com/sites/laurenorsini/2017/08/31/ catching-up-on-yuri-on-ice-with-figure-skater-johnny-weir/.

41. yoiconph, "Don't Stop Us Now, the Moment of Truth! Like Http://Facebook.Com /Yoiconph for More Information! Pic.Twitter.Com/QeOsOdI39H," Tweet, @

yoiconph via Twitter (blog), December 22, 2016, https://twitter.com/yoiconph/status/811940043862380544.

42. *Yuri on Ice!!!* Only events were also held in Indonesia (yoiconid, 2017) and Singapore (yoiconsg, 2017–18).

43. Yoizine PH Team, *Tara Na! [Let's Go!]* (Manila, Philippines: Self-published, 2018), 2.

44. Yoizine PH Team, 2.

45. Tanaw, "The Sound Of," *Toranoana,* https://ec.toranoana.shop/joshi/ec/item/040030542803/ (accessed June 10, 2018).

In Front of the Law

The Production and Distribution of Boys' Love Dôjinshi in Indonesia

NICE HUANG

By the recession in the 1990s, Japan's social structure had changed from an economic superpower to a cool cultural country.[1] In order to promote their new image as "a cool country," the Japanese government introduced a political strategy called "Cool Japan" in 2002, which has successfully boosted anime, manga, and video games exports.[2] Since then, the anime and manga industries have become the face of Japan's popular culture. Not only have these art forms managed to spread globally but the subcultures of these cultural industries—such as dôjinshi comics and cosplay—have also successfully penetrated other countries' markets. Dôjinshi as a fan work, the parody of an original manga or anime work, motivates fans to imagine how the original story might be retold. This might be one reason why manga industries persist and are growing strong both in Japan and globally. One genre that had been growing exponentially from this subculture is a branch of the shôjo genre, a male homosexual romance subgenre known as "Boys' Love" (BL). With the rise in the number of fans for popular shônen works, such as the *Captain Tsubasa* and *Gundam* series, female fans began producing homosexual parodies of those series' male characters in sexual relationships.

As subcultures, both BL and dôjinshi amateur manga have been spreading rapidly to other countries. Other than its home country of Japan, the United States, and Europe are perhaps the key areas that have been prodigiously producing BL dôjinshi manga, merchandise, and events. It may also be because these parts of the world have been more open to homosexual relationships and even same-sex marriage. But, surprisingly, for some countries that openly reject the notions of homosexual relationships, either by their law or culture, this kind of market activity still manages to exist. Indonesia is one of these countries. Even if Indonesia is not an Islamic country, the majority of this country would agree that homosexuality is a sin. It does not help that the government and the media are framing LGBT people as abnormal and sexually addicted by focusing on their sexual activities.[3] This opinion has been written into the application of Law no. 44/2008 on Pornography, the purpose of which is to "prevent the development of pornography and sex commercialization in society."[4] Unfortunately, pornography in this law defined as "indecent or sexual exploitation that violates moral norms in society,"[5] a definition that could be interpreted in many ways. By using such an unreliable definition, there is a high risk that bias against the subject will interfere in the judgment of law. The misuses of this law can be seen in many cases where gay people in Indonesia have been arrested because of their sexuality and the stereotypes around it.[6] Discrimination against LGBT subjects by using the law on pornography also extends to digital world. Guided by this law, the Ministry of Communication and Information proposed and executed the "Internet Healthy" program, in which they blocked many LGBT dating apps for smartphones, pressuring digital comic websites such as LINE Webtoon, Comica, and Ciayo to take down any works with an LGBT nuance, and blocked many websites such as Reddit, Vimeo, and Tumblr[7] because of the unfiltered LGBT and pornographic content that they allegedly contain. In this harsh environment, it is surprising that BL dôjinshi managed to enter the market and actually develop in Indonesia.

The existence of BL in Indonesia has been noted by many researchers, but most were focused on the readers and the genre itself.[8] Despite the increasing number of anime and manga convention events in Indonesia, which were also encouraging local artists to sell their dôjinshi works, there was little information about the local BL dôjinshi market and its distribution. Yamila Abraham, founder of the publishing company of Yaoi Press and a BL writer, has noticed the potential market for homoerotic and romance stories in Indonesia, but feels that creators must conceal themselves from the public for their own safety because of the strict conservative view regarding erotic and homosexual content. While the internet helped with the proliferation of BL works in Indonesia, in which there was loose control over the digital and printed distribution of such materials, Abraham expressed her concern that this subgenre would not have a long life in Indonesia.[9]

Given such strict yet ambiguous regulations about homosexuality in Indonesia, this essay investigates how Indonesian dôjinshi artists (*dôjinka*) are navigating through the antipornography laws in the process of publishing and distributing their BL works. Analyzing personal testimonies gathered through interviews with four Indonesian female dôjinka via Twitter and Skype, I compare the BL dôjinshi cultures in both Japan and Indonesia and explain how Indonesian dôjinka are producing their BL dôjinshi in Indonesia.

Boys' Love Dôjinshi Culture in Japan and Indonesia

The industries of anime and manga in Japan are so powerful that despite the burst of the "Cool Japan" bubble, they are still being created, exported, and consumed in other countries. When looking closely, it is clear that the activity on the amateur side of those industries is still prolific in Japan as well, with many events, such as Comic Market (Comiket) or (Super) Comic City held as amateur markets every year. These are events where people purchase and sell the products that are produced by not only amateurs but also professionals who might temporarily operate as amateurs under a different name. The products themselves are called *nijisôsaku*, which explains the product itself as a fan-made derivation or spin-off products from an original work. They may take shape as goods such as key chains, fanart posters, file holders, and accessories, or as dôjinshi. Even so, Kania A. Sukotjo, an Indonesian media and BL researcher, explains that the main purpose for people who come to such events in Japan is to purchase the dôjinshi. Sukotjo points out that the visitors of such events can purchase so many dôjinshi at a time—as many as forty books—that they need to prepare a big tote bag beforehand.[10]

The dôjinshi itself was originally defined by the Japan's Comic Market committee as "magazines published as a cooperative effort by a group of individuals who share a common ideology or goals with the aim of establishing a medium through which their works can be presented," and has been treated as a medium for fans to express their love of one original work.[11] While this definition gives the impression that dôjinshi are limited to printed goods using "published magazines" as its original media, dôjinshi has also spread to digital formats. Toranoana, a bookstore that provides dôjinshi from various circles of dôjinka, also provides spaces for digital dôjinshi consumption, even though in smaller numbers. For example, on April 29, 2018, there were 65 dôjinshi titles derived from *Yuri!!! on Ice* that were put on Toranoana's online store as digital dôjinshi, compared to the 300 titles of printed dôjinshi from the same fandom. We could also see an overwhelming gap in the *Osomatsu-san* fandom, in which there was 16,443 titles of printed dôjinshi and only 209 titles in digital formats. Even though there are just a few digital dôjinshi in the online bookstore, the number of digital dôjinshi that are being shared for free is considerable. This is because many dôjinshi artists are also sharing their works (either as short comics, fan art, or as a teaser of the dôjinshi they are going to sell) to promote themselves on social media or digital art platforms.

Dôjinshi are published in various formats. Many dôjinshi have been published on A5 paper size, but the size has varied, unlike manga, which usually sticks to the B6 paper size. The difference in formatting could be accounted for in the structure of the publishing process of dôjinshi. Whereas manga are processed professionally by publishers that have a certain standard for the genre, the amateur published dôjinshi are processed without having to conform to any publisher's rules and standards. Thus, the dôjinka can publish their work according to their own design or budget. With this freedom, the more famous dôjinka sometimes publish compilation books of their previous stories as exclusive editions, a feat that would be hard to publish as a regular manga. Added embellishments such a metallic gold on the edge of the paper, for the exclusivity effect prized by collectors, raises the cost beyond the usual price of dôjinshi. Of course, because dôjinshi are handled within a personal budget, produced in a customized size and made in smaller numbers than manga, the production cost of dôjinshi is generally higher than for manga, which also translates to selling at higher price. A 40-page dôjinshi usually sells for around 1000 yen, while a 200-page manga is generally sold for around 500–700 yen. But despite being usually more expensive than manga, the market for dôjinshi seems not have weakened. Instead, the committee of Comiket has recorded a gradual increase in the number of circle participants, going from 700 circles in 1975 to 32,000 in December 2017.[12]

As one of the dominating genres in the market of dôjinshi, BL—known more commonly as *yaoi* outside of Japan—is a subgenre of shôjo that become an umbrella term for male homoerotic products. Even though BL are stories of male–male homoerotica, this genre mainly relies on heterosexist values, in which the couples are depicted within stereotypical male/female relationships.[13] This genre targets female readers, who are known as *fujoshi* or "rotten women," and it has become quite a phenomenon among the otaku fandom. Some researchers such as Ueno Chizuko and Fujimoto Yukari believe that the consummation of this male–male homoerotic genre provides an escape for the readers, especially women, from the limitations of patriarchal society by allowing them to play with gender and sex freely.[14] On the other hand, some researchers such as Mark McLelland, Patrick Galbraith, and Rachel Matt Thorn argue that fujoshi do not care about the political possibilities mentioned by these researchers and only pursue the pleasure of consummation and their fantasy.[15] Even though much research has been conducted to explain the content and readers of this genre, there is still not enough research on its other aspects, such as its male readers (fudanshi or "rotten men").[16]

Suzuki Midori explains that the BL genre itself has existed since the early

Comic Markets in the 1970s, when the popularity of the shônen-ai genre was booming.[17] The production of male–male relationship dôjinshi was then intensified with the popularity of shônen genre manga in the 1980s and '90s, such as *Captain Tsubasa, Neon Genesis Evangelion*, the *Gundam* series, *Slam Dunk*, and others, among female fans. Considering that the shônen genre's main theme is the emotional bonds between male characters (i.e., rivalry, friendship, and teamwork), it is not unexpected for fujoshi to read those bonds as containing potential homosexual relationships, and consequently create spin-off dôjinshi about their favorite characters. This kind of tension between male characters that fujoshi love has permeated to the professional side of the industry as one kind of fan service to accommodate female customers in order to raise the popularity of shônen manga. This, of course, strengthens and boosts the market for dôjinshi, especially BL dôjinshi, which has already existed for quite some time. The results of using homoerotic content to target female fans can be seen in the survey results published by the Comic Market Preparation Committee in which 71 percent of participating circles and 57 percent of visitors of Comiket were female.[18]

This suggests that the economic market that is proliferating in Japan is being approved in some ways by the professional side of the anime and manga industries and, to a certain extent, the government. Even though the stories in dôjinshi place amateur creators in potentially compromised positions by using copyrighted characters from an original work, most professional mangaka and publishers tend not sue for this activity as an infringement of copyright. In some cases, dôjinka were even scouted by manga publishers and have managed to obtain a professional debut.[19] Popular mangaka such as Takahashi Rumiko, CLAMP, and Hoshino Katsura among others, are some of the examples.

While dôjinshi culture is spreading its wings globally, there is little published work about dôjinshi culture in Indonesia. In Indonesia, Comiket can be traced back as early as 1990.[20] At the time, Indonesia's Comiket was not an independent event like Japan's Comiket. Early Comikets in Indonesia were miniature versions of the Japanese Comiket that only were held as part of Japanese cultural events. Many of these events were held by communities that were focusing on Japanese culture, such as Fusion Matsuri Bina Nusantara University in 2006 or the annual event Gelar Jepang Universitas Indonesia (GJUI). The most notable among them was a Japanese culture event called Animonster Sound J-I Matsuri in 2006, which was held by Animonster, a popular Japanese culture magazine in Indonesia that focused on anime and manga. A group called Dôjinshi Indonesia considers the Animonster Sound J-I Matsuri in 2006 as the first Comiket in Indonesia, even though it was held as a part of larger Japanese cultural event like the other mini Comikets.[21] Dôjinshi Indonesia already acknowledged the existence of BL audiences in Indonesia from the start by allowing its members to submit BL dôjinshi and welcoming all genres in the event. This integration of Comiket with Japanese cultural events persisted well into the 2010s. Sukotjo's analysis of anime and manga convention events in Surabaya, Indonesia, explains how these Indonesian events are similar yet also different from comic conventions in Tokyo. She explains that, in Tokyo, people put dôjinshi as their highest priority for attending, whereas in Indonesia, the event acts not only as a marketplace for dôjinshi and original comic consumption but also as a place for other activities, such as cosplay. Despite this, according to Sukotjo's research, both Tokyo's and Surabaya's events have the same purpose: to create a safe space for anime and manga lovers, specifically BL fans, to express their love towards the fandom.[22] The popularity of Comiket events became known nationally when AFA (Anime Festival Asia) 2012 was held in Jakarta. After that, national anime and comic conventions such as Comifuro (Comic Frontier) in 2013 and Indonesian Comic-Con in 2015 began to be held annually. This development also gave anime and manga fans from other provinces an incentive to hold similar events in their city.

As Sukotjo has pointed out, Comiket in Indonesia mostly follow the same format and procedures as their Japanese equivalent, such as dividing up the individual booths based on fandoms and/or genre. However, BL dôjinshi in Indonesian Comikets are affected by a special rule regarding their distribution. Starting in 2006, this rule was promoted by the Dôjinshi Indonesia group to prevent any problems with the government and mainstream society and as a reaction to the antipornography laws designed by the parliament at that time.[23] The rule states that any dôjinshi or original comic that contains any "dangerous" or adult intimate scenes must be sealed by wrapping it with plastic and must not be opened at the convention site. Also, any products with such scenes on the cover cannot be displayed on the tables, even though they can be registered in the event's product catalogue. This rule was still being applied as of 2018.

In terms of the market, printed dôjinshi in Indonesia have been visibly growing thanks to these annual comic conventions. While this means that dôjinka in Indonesia still rely heavily on comic convention events for sales and distribution, it does not mean that they are lacking in terms of digital dôjinshi. Using websites such as Fanfiction.net, Wattpad, Archive of Our Own,

Deviant Art, Tumblr, and Patreon for fan works, fans from Indonesia are increasingly distributing their work online. One main obstacle for the present research is the fact that it is very difficult to keep track how many Indonesians are actually sharing BL dôjinshi on the internet, as many of them publish their works in English so as not to expose their nationality.

Navigating Through the Law

In order to examine the condition of local artists who publish homoerotic works, and how the law is affecting them in the process of production and distribution, I have conducted interviews with four Indonesian female comic artists via Twitter and Skype (Figure 1). The respondents ranged from twenty to thirty years old. Two of them were undergraduate students (A and B), one of them was self-employed (C), and the other was a freelance artist (D). While three of them were highly experienced in the field of BL printed dôjinshi and have published 7–10 titles of dôjinshi, one of them (A) was a beginner who had just published her debut dôjinshi.

Despite the bias toward homosexuality and the antipornography law in Indonesia, the four respondents did not have any trouble finding willing printing companies for their works. Two of them (A and B) were going to the same printing company to print their dôjinshi at the time of the interview. Two of them (A and B) got the information of the willing printing company from their friends who had prior experiences with the company. One of them (C) was given a suggestion by her family driver, and the other (D) already knew of a willing printing company from her university experience. The printing staff themselves handled the order professionally. They did not make any comment regarding the content of customer's works when checking and setting it for print. They only commented on the difficulty of drawing a comic and were curious about the reason behind the high numbers of copies that the customer had ordered. This suggests that those printing companies possibly prioritized economic profit over their potential social bias. Given the fact that LGBT people in Indonesia have been discriminated against based on their sexuality, it was surprising that the respondents' works, which contain homosexual nuances, were not being rejected or reported. It must be noted that the four respondents were not printing any sexual scenes in their dôjinshi in Indonesia, so even if the staff had been a doing quick check on the soft copies and printed results, it is questionable whether they could have stumbled on

Respondent	A	B	C	D
Age	20s	20	25–30	26
Occupation	Undergraduate student	Undergraduate student	Self-employed	Freelance artist
Published dôjinshi(s)	1 book, 0 digital	8 books, 2 digital	11 books, 4 digital	7 books, 2 digital
Local printing company information	Recommended by her friend	Recommended by other local dôjinka	Recommended by her family driver	Found by herself near her alma mater university
Published for international market	No	Yes	Yes	Yes
Published on Toranoana	No	Yes	No	Yes
Published R-18 dôjinshi for local market	No	No	No	No
Published R-18 dôjinshi for international market	No	Yes	Yes	Yes
Join local comic market	Yes	Yes	Yes	Yes
Join international comic market	No	Yes	Yes	Yes
Digital shop	None	Gumroad	Email	Sellfy, Patreon
Separating private life from the BL fandom and dôjinka life	Yes	Yes	Yes	Yes
Hiding identity as BL fan and dôjinka	Yes	Yes	Yes	Yes
Have someone to help in production	Yes, friends (familiar with BL)	Yes, friends (familiar with BL) and family (unfamiliar with BL)	Yes, friends (familiar with BL)	No

Figure 1. Summary of respondents' interview data.

scenes with homosexual nuance and/or whether they were familiar with and understood such contents.

The printing companies that the four respondents were using each have their own websites to promote their services. These websites offered no details about their comic-printing service, only information concerning their service for printing books. Indonesian artists who want to print their dôjinshi must contact the printing company to negotiate conditions. This situation is the opposite of that in Japan, where printing companies list many types of services for printing dôjinshi or comic on their websites. Such differences might reflect different opinions toward comic production and their content. The amateur comic industry is seen as a serious business in Japan, whereas in Indonesia the publishing of comics is still not considered as having business potential. Additionally, Indonesia is generally moving from printed works to digital works. Especially for comics, there is a large tendency to obtain them freely but illegally from manga scanlation websites.

Not all printing companies in Indonesia are willing to accept job orders from BL artists. One of my informants (C) described a friend's experiences wherein her comic had been rejected. Usually the company would ignore the email or message as their expression of rejection, but the worst case was literally being chased out from the printing company's office because of her proposed content. Certainly, we understand there was, and is, a divided opinion in Indonesian printing companies regarding this kind of order.

Interestingly, three of the experienced informants (B, C, and D) have printed and published their works in Japan. Two of them (B and D) were contacted directly by Toranoana, which offered to translate and print their works in Japan, on the condition that the dôjinshi must be sold exclusively in Toranoana shops. Respondent D said that Japanese publishers might have seen their art on Pixiv (a Japanese amateur art website) before deciding to contact her. BL researchers and editors have also observed that the editors of manga publishers in Japan were often on the digital lookout for the potential artists and art to be published with their company.[24] Respondent D also used this chance to publish dôjinshi with intimate homosexual scenes. Three of the respondents (B, C, D) had developed a global customer base by promoting their art and ideas beforehand on their blogs and social networks. Their works are sold and distributed not only in Japan but also internationally. This indicates how much the potential of Indonesian comic artists has escalated, especially within the BL comic world.

In terms of content, style, and material for printing their works, all four of the respondents used Japanese dôjinshi as their standard. They preferred the A5 or B5 paper size not only because it is the common size of dôjinshi in Japan but also because they felt that it is the proper size to accommodate their art. They especially avoided the grayish scrap paper that Indonesian comic publishers usually use, because of its lower quality than what the Japanese industry was using for comics. Respondent D explained that Indonesian printing companies did not paper with same quality as in Japan, so she negotiated for the Japanese standard by using HVS 100gram paper as her media. Other artists also expressed similar concerns because they wanted to produce works with a similar quality as Japan's dôjinshi. Because of the standard they used for their works, and the low number of printing orders (in comparison with the number of comics that were being published by Indonesian comic publishers), the production cost of dôjinshi was higher, thus the price of dô-jinshi in Indonesia was higher than the usual comics, mirroring the condition of Japan's dôjinshi.

The composition of the dôjinshi they made was also based on the format of manga, as manga has strongly influenced Indonesian comic practice. In the 1990s, there was a manga boom in Indonesia. Many titles, such as *Candy Candy, Doraemon, Kungfu Boy*, and others, were published and have since successfully created Japan's manga fanbase.[25] Due to their popularity, manga in Indonesia then began to replace American comics, which had been shrinking in production. From November 2017 to January 2018, Elex Media Komputindo, one of largest comics publishers in Indonesia, did not publish any Western comics. Out of 50 comics that have been published by Elex, 48 were manga and 2 were Korean manhwa.[26] The domination of manga has changed the public's perception of comics in Indonesia. While simple formats, such as four-panel comic strips, could still be found, Indonesians found themselves more familiar with the manga format. The comic publishers themselves began to accommodate to manga's right-to-left reading format to appeal to manga fans.[27]

The access to manga and BL genres from Japan was still open in Indonesia. Even though BL dôjinshi imported from Japan are not allowed in Indonesia, illegal translated dôjinshi and manga (called scanlations) can be easily accessed by anyone with an internet connection. Also, one branch of the Japanese bookstore chain Kinokuniya in Jakarta managed to put untranslated BL manga and light novels on their shelf, albeit in small numbers, though not on the front shelves. While only two of the respondents (C and B) have physically been to Japan, the network that they have built with other comic artists and the BL fandom easily gave them access to information on dôjinshi elements and format.

Regarding the publishing process, D was the only respondent doing all the work on her own. The other respondents had friends familiar with BL to help them out. Informant B even had her family and one close friend who were not familiar with the BL genre help with the distribution process. Though the artists had been open with their friends, none of them decided to disclose their activities and works as BL dôjinka to their family, and they all limited the number of friends who knew about it. This reveals how the artists feel that the discrepancy between their love for BL dôjinshi and societal norms was still strong and decided to avoid confrontation. This is similar to what Sukotjo has noted about the participants of BL comic events in Indonesia, where they were willing to negotiate their moral norms.[28]

With the existence of international customers and the opportunities to join international comic conventions in other countries such as Singapore or Philippines, three of my respondents had shipped their printed works to other countries, and/or carried it in their suitcases when they traveled. Given how aggressively the antipornography law has been applied, there were many reports by local newspapers, such as Detik News and Jawa Pos, where customs had confiscated pornographic materials such as DVDs and magazines.[29] Somehow, despite the oppositional view and strict screening that Indonesia has toward pornography and homosexuality, my respondents never faced problems while they were distributing it via mail or carrying it in their suitcase. We can see that the law in Indonesia, especially the antipornography law that has been used to antagonize LGBT people, is inconsistently enforced. Also, the stereotype of comics in Indonesia might be one of reasons why they were safe bringing their works. Comics, in the majority of Indonesian's mindset, are reading material for children, which results in a presumption that the story will not breach societal norms and is safe for consumption.

Within the bounds of the events in which my informants had participated as sellers, BL dôjinshi were being sold freely in Indonesia. They confirmed that the committees in charge of the events were aware of economic transactions of BL dôjinshi and art works by its participants. In Indonesia, the committees themselves had shown no negative reaction toward such goods, but dôjinshi with sexual content or R-18 ratings must be wrapped in plastic and, depending on the event, must be kept under the tables. In general, the customers already know of the existence of such dôjinshi beforehand and know how to purchase it. The customers can preorder it or express their wish to purchase the R-18 dôjinshi to the seller. Even so, I doubt that many of the venue owners or staff were aware of the commercial transactions that were happening at these events. My doubt was confirmed by respondent C's statement during our interview: "And if the venue owner knew what kind of goods were being sold at the dôjin[shi] event, there would be a problem" ("dan kalo penyedia venue tahu tema barang2 yg dijual di event dôjin, bisa dipermasalahkan").[30]

Three of my respondents (B, C, and D) were also selling dôjinshi in digital formats. Respondents B and C were offering their works as digital versions (PDF format in their case) available by request only. D was putting her old works on an online shop as the last chance for her customers to buy the works before removing them from the market. While they were using different methods to manage the transactions, they only put their old works in their "shop." As C was limited to "request only," the transactions were done personally via email, without the use of any website services. B and D were using artist website services such as Patreon, Sellfy, and Gumroad to manage their transactions. Sellfy and Gumroad allow the artists to track who can download and read the dôjinshi, thus lowering the chance of plagiarism, a common problem of the digital arts and comic world. As those websites were based outside Indonesia, the artists could post their adult-themed works without being afraid of repercussions from the Indonesian government.

For sharing their fan art and promoting their dôjinshi works, all of my respondents chose to separate their private account from their art account. D even went so far as to not mention that she was Indonesian in order to avoid any connection to her private life. This was one of the strategies the artists used to escape the legal restrictions in their home country. With the protection of the digital world, they felt safer selling their works digitally. Some of the reasons why they prefer to publish their work digitally include lower costs and effort, but also fewer chances for social or legal problems to occur, as they are not forced into contact with outsiders, such as printing companies that are usually homophobic. Even so, D noted that dôjinshi culture in Indonesia was still a heavily print-based comic market, and events still held potential economic merit for local dôjinka.

Overall, all four of my informants were aware that the genre of their works was not acceptable in Indonesia because of the biased view toward homosexuality. However, all of them thought that their BL works were not breaking any Indonesian law. When I mentioned the antipornography law that has been used as the main law to antagonize homosexuality in Indonesia, three of them (A, B, and C) mentioned the ambiguity and loopholes in the law itself. Respondent D stressed the strong bias toward homosexuality, especially from left-wing parties and organizations. She also mentioned that, at a time when the tension regarding LGBT issues had been high, she and her friends, who are also fujoshi, were really concerned about what would happen if such parties and organizations suddenly came to inspect goods in the comic dôjinshi event: "Yes, there was a panic back then (when the extremist Islamic Party inspections and raids frequently happened). My friends, who are fujoshi, were panicking on social media. 'Ugh, what will happen to us? What if [they come to] inspect [the comic market event]?'" ("Iya, sempat. Sempet kemarin tuh keter-keter lho, orang-orang, temen-temen di mana, social media tuh, yang fujoshi-fujoshi. 'Ih, gimana nanti kita? (Kalau) digerebek gimana?")[31] Even if a lot of artists and fans of this genre feel that there were no consequences because of their activities and relaxed enforcement of an ambiguous law, the fear of confrontation with the government and society persists.

Conclusion

Boys' Love dôjinshi, as one of Japan's manga subcultures that managed to expand globally, has also been growing in conservative countries such as Indonesia. Despite the strong bias and laws that were being used against it, BL distribution and production in Indonesia is growing. While such activities already existed in the late 1990s, anime and comic convention events and other free spaces for such works have boomed in popularity since 2012, growing stronger with its annual national events. The promising Indonesian market has not only received products and influences from Japan as the subculture's origin country but also managed to create a reverse flow of distribution from Indonesia to Japan with quality similar to Japanese dôjinshi.

Despite the strong bias and ambiguous laws that are being used to antagonize homosexuality and pornography, the legislation itself did not have any effects on this subculture, aside from causing some anxiety. There are three reasons for this situation. First, comics themselves are still regarded as children's reading material and their economic potential has not been seen as a serious business in Indonesia. Second, BL and dôjinshi were still categorized as subcultural products in Indonesia, and thus have not gained enough visibility to be judged by mainstream society. Unlike some anime such as *Crayon Shin-chan*, which has high visibility and thus was banned from Indonesian television because of its display of inappropriate manners,[32] BL dôjinshi are still limited to more private transactions such as comic events, preorder systems, and media accounts. And third, the economic potential that this subculture brought was prioritized by other parties like printing companies, event committees, and venue owners who have a stake in the production and distribution process of the dôjinshi. Even if the printing companies and the owner of venues might not be aware of what goods were being sold, the profit and merit they gained from this fan activity offers a strong incentive to maintain it.

There are two strategies used by my respondents to evade the antipornography law. The first strategy is avoiding intimate expressions in works that were sold locally. This does not mean that the artists did not publish any adult scenes in their works, but they only published their works with such scenes secretly or outside of Indonesia, or on other countries' servers and websites. The other strategy is separating their private lives from their lives as BL dôjinka. This was done either by hiding their activities from their family and friends or by hiding their nationality from their audiences and customers.

Seeing how much some BL dôjinshi comic artists in Indonesia have progressed globally, and how the comic convention events are growing as its safe market space, BL dôjinshi in Indonesia seems to be growing stronger as an invisible subculture regardless of the present strong oppositional view toward LGBT people. Nevertheless, we cannot ignore the fact that BL has a subversive potential and can change the reader's stance toward homosexuality. The four informants in this paper have an open and tolerant stance toward LGBT people by producing dôjinshi with LGBT contents and criticizing the implementation of the antipornography law based merely on social prejudice. Furthermore, the online questionnaire in August 21, 2018, by *Buku Pintar BL*, a BL database in Indonesia, revealed that BL provides more insights and knowledge regarding LGBT culture to Indonesian readers.[33] Even though Indonesian BL fans and readers still have an inner struggle between a religion that condemns LGBT and their interest in this subculture,[34] Indonesian BL fans have become more open and tolerant toward LGBT people in general.[35] But do BL media in Indonesia have the power to change the oppositional and conservative opinion outside of Indonesian otaku community? Looking at the current situation where LGBT-related contents in Indonesia must hide their presence from public, to answer this question with affirmative may sound laughable. Yet, with the growth of BL culture in Indonesia and the subversive potential that BL has, BL can contribute as one factor to influence Indonesian society to be more tolerant towards the LGBT community.

···

Nice Huang is a master's student in Gender Studies at the Humanities Department of Nagoya University. Her research is focusing on Japanese pop culture, Boys' Love genre, gender, and fan studies. Currently, her research involves the depiction of queer relationship in *Yuri!!! on Ice* and the interaction between real life athletes and anime fans.

···

Notes

1. Douglas McGray, "Japan's Gross National Cool," *Foreign Policy*, November 11, 2009, https://foreignpolicy.com/2009/11/11/japans-gross-national-cool/.

2. Michal Daliot-Bul, "Japan Brand Strategy: The Taming of 'Cool Japan' and the Challenges of Cultural Planning in a Postmodern Age," *Social Science Japan Journal* 12, no. 2 (2009): 247–49.

3. Jobpie Sugiharto, "Dikecam Soal LGBT, Menteri Nasir: Karena Kurang Seks (Criticized for His Remarks About LGBT, Minister Nasir: Because It Lacked the Sex)," *Tempo*, January 25, 2016, https://nasional.tempo.co/read/739204/dikecam-soal-lgbt-menteri-nasir-karena-kurang-seks. Masfiatur Rochma, "Pelaku Pesta Seks Kaum Gay di Surabaya Divonis 2,5 Tahun Bui" (The Perpetrators of Gay Sex Party in Surabaya Sentenced to Prison for 2,5 Years)," *Merdeka*, September 19, 2017, https://www.merdeka.com/peristiwa/pelaku-pesta-seks-kaum-gay-di-surabaya-divonis-25-tahun-bui.html. Muhammad Sholeh, "FPKS sebut pesta seks gay di Jakut jadi tanda Indonesia darurat LGBT" (FPKS Said That Gay Sex Party in North Jakarta Is a Sign That Indonesia Is Facing LGBT Crisis)," *Merdeka*, May 23, 2017, https://www.merdeka.com/peristiwa/fpks-sebut-pesta-seks-gay-di-jakut-jadi-tanda-indonesia-darurat-lgbt.html.

4. *Undang-undang Republik Indonesia Nomor 44 Tahun 2008 tentang Pornografi* (Law no. 44 of 2008 on Pornography), chapter 1, article 3, point e (my translation) (Indonesia: Indonesian Government, 2008).

5. *Undang-undang Republik Indonesia Nomor 44 Tahun 2008 tentang Pornografi* (Law no. 44 of 2008 on Pornography), chapter 1, article 1, no. 1 (my translation) (Indonesia: Indonesian Government, 2008).

6. Vincent Bevins, "It's Not Illegal to be Gay in Indonesia, But Police Are Cracking Down Anyway," *The Washington Post*, October 12, 2017, https://www.washingtonpost.com/news/worldviews/wp/2017/10/12/its-not-illegal-to-be-gay-in-indonesia-but-police-are-cracking-down-anyway/?utm_term=.48ec4e732c6d.

7. "Internet Sehat dan Aman (INSAN)I (Healthy and Safe Internet)," *Kementrian Komunikasi dan Informatika Republik Indonesia*, last modified October 23, 2013, https://www.kominfo.go.id/content/detail/3303/internet-sehat-dan-aman-insan/0/internet_sehat. Desi Setyowati, "Kominfo Minta Google Cabut 73 Aplikasi LGBT dari Play Store (Ministry of Information and Communication Asks Google to Delete 73 LGBT Applications from Play Store)," *Kata Data*, January 22, 2018, https://katadata.co.id/berita/2018/01/22/kominfo-minta-google-cabut-73-aplikasi-lgbt-dari-play-store. Aprilkurnia, "Baca Komik Gratis Lewat COMICA (Read Free Comics With COMICA)," last modified April 11, 2017, https://comicstogi.wordpress.com/2017/04/11/baca-komik-gratis-lewat-comica. Agung Bintoro, "Kominfo Akui Pemblokiran Tumblr (Ministry of Information and Communication Acknowledges to Have Blocked Tumblr)," *CNN Indonesia*, March 6, 2018, https://www.cnnindonesia.com/teknologi/20180306121701-185-280789/kominfo-akui-pemblokiran-tumblr.

8. Dara Ayudyasari and Welly Wirman, "Konstruksi Makna Gay Bagi Penggemar Manga Yaoi (Fujoshi) pada Anggota Komunitas Otaku di Pekanbaru (The Construction of Gay Definition for Yaoi Manga Fans (Fujoshi) in Pekanbaru's Otaku Community Members)," *Jurnal Online Mahasiswa Fakultas Ilmu Sosial dan Ilmu Politik Universitas Riau* 13, no. 2 (October 2016): 1–15, https://www.neliti.com/publications/133806/konstruksi-makna-gay-bagi-penggemar-manga-yaoi-fujoshi-pada-anggota-komunitas-ot. Putri Andam Dewi, "Komunitas Fujoshi di Kalangan Perempuan Indonesia (Fujoshi Community in Indonesian Women)," *Lingua Cultura* 6, no. 2 (2012): 173–82, http://journal.binus.ac.id/index.php/Lingua/article/download/404/384. Septia Winduwati, "Fujoshi Remaja dan Kenikmatan Bermedia Yaoi: Studi Kasus pada Remaja Putri Penggemar Fiksi Romantis Homoerotis Jepang (Teenager Fujoshi and the Pleasure to Do Yaoi in Media: A Study Case of Female Teenager Fans of Japanese Romantic Homoerotic Story)," 2015, http://repository.untar.ac.id/426/1/2089-4551-2-PB.pdf.

9. Yamilla Abraham, "Boys' Love Thrives in Conservative Indonesia," in *Boys' Love Manga: Essays on the Sexual Ambiguity and Cross-Cultural Fandom of the Genre*, ed. Levi Antonia, Mark McHarry, Dru Pagliassotti (Jefferson, N.C.: McFarland & Company, Inc., 2008), 51–52.

10. Kania A. Sukotjo, "Expression of Love on Yaoi Content in Tokyo and Surabaya Comic Events," paper presented at Proceedings of the 9th Next Generation Global Workshop, Kyoto University Asian Studies Unit, Kyoto, March 2017, 306, http://www.kuasu.cpier.kyoto-u.ac.jp/wp-content/uploads/2017/03/8-2.Kania-Arini-Sukotjo_20160910.pdf.

11. Comic Market Preparation Committee, "What is the Comic Market?" (February 2008), 3, http://www.comiket.co.jp/info-a/WhatIsEng080225.pdf.

12. Komikku Mâketto Junbikai, *40th Comic Market Chronicle* (Tokyo: Kyôshin Insatsu Kabushiki Gaisha, 2015), 28, 328; *Komikku Mâketto Nenpyō* (Comic Market Chronological Table). Komikku Mâketto Nenpyō, https://www.comiket.co.jp/archives/Chronology.html#graph_area (accessed September 20, 2018).

13. Febriani Sihombing, "On the Iconic Difference Between Couple Characters in Boys Love Manga," *Image & Narrative* 12, no. 1 (2011), http://www.imageandnarrative.be/index.php/imagenarrative/article/viewFile/130/101"&gt.

14. Chizuko Ueno, "Jendâresu Wârudo no Jikken (The Experiment of Genderless World)," in *Hatshujô Sochi: Erosu no Shinario* (Tokyo: Chikuma Shobo, 1998), 131; Yukari Fujimoto, *Watashi no Ibasho wa Doko ni Aruno: Shōjo Manga ga Utsusu Kokoro no Katachi* (Where Is the Place I Belong To? The Forms of Heart That Projects Shôjo Manga) (Tokyo: Gakuyo Shobô, 1998), 140–41.

15. Patrick W. Galbraith, "Fujoshi: Fantasy Play and Transgressive Intimacy Among 'Rotten Girls' in Contemporary Japan," *Signs: Journal of Women in Culture and Society* 37, no. 1 (2017). www.jstor.org/stable/10.1086/660182; Mark McLelland, "Why are Japanese Girls' Comics Full of Boys Bonking?" *Intensities: The Journal of Cult Media* 1 (December 2012), https://intensitiescultmedia.files.wordpress.com

/2012/12/mclelland.pdf; Rachel Matt Thorn, "Girls and Women Getting Out of Hand: The Pleasure and Politics of Japan's Amateur Comics Community," in *Fanning the Flames: Fans and Consumer Culture in Contemporary Japan*, ed. William W. Kelly (Albany: State University of New York Press, 2004), 169–87.

16. Nagaike Kazumi, "Queer Readings of BL: Are Women "Plunderes" of Gay Men?" in *International Perspectives on Shôjo and Shôjo Manga: The Influence of Girl Culture*, ed. Masami Toku (New York: Routledge, 2015), https://books.google.co.jp/books?hl=en&lr=&id=tFLLCQAAQBAJ&oi=fnd&pg=PT88&dq=fudanhi&ots=qFsVV1Rk67&sig=cMadIfopPMM_mCenh4z8kLYYuJk#v=onepage&q=fudanshi&f=false.

17. Midori Suzuki, "The Possibilities of Research on Fujoshi in Japan," in *Transnational Boys' Love Fan Studies* 12 (2013), ed. Nagaike Kazumi and Suganuma Katsuhiko, http://dx.doi.org/10.3983/twc.2013.0462.

18. Comic Market Preparation Committee, "What is The Comic Market?" 21.

19. Kaneda Junko, Fukuda Rika, and Yamamoto Fumiko, "Atsuki Boizu Rabu no Hyôgen o Kataru Moeru Soudankai (A Moe Meeting to Discuss the Expression of Passionate Boy's Love)," Interview, *Bijutsu Techo Boizu Rabu*, December 2014, 72.

20. Abraham, "Boys' Love Thrives," 51.

21. Bayô-kun, "Comiket Plan! (Issue 1)," https://dôjinshiindonesia.deviantart.com/journal/Comiket-Plan-Issue-1-249263321 (accessed May 2, 2018).

22. Sukotjo, "Expression of Love," 310–11.

23. Bayô-kun, "Comiket Plan (Issue 3) UPDATE!" https://www.deviantart.com/doujinshiindonesia/journal/Comiket-Plan-Issue-3-UPDATE-249897613 (accessed May 2, 2018).

24. Kaneda, Fukuda, and Yamamoto, "Atsuki Boizu Rabu," 72.

25. Putri Andam Dewi, "Budaya Manga: Pengaruh Budaya Manga di Kalangan Anak Muda Indonesia (Manga Culture: The Influence of Manga Towards Indonesian Youth)," (n.d.), 2, https://www.academia.edu/9175298/Budaya_Manga_di_kalangan_Remaja_Indonesia (accessed January 27, 2018).

26. "Elex Kategori Komik (Elex Comic Category)," Elex Media Komputindo, http://elexmedia.id/users/kategori_komik (accessed 26 January 2018).

27. Kristine M. Santos and Febriani Sihombing, "Cool Manga in Indonesia and the Philippines," in *The End of Cool Japan: Ethical, Legal, and Cultural Challenges to Japanese Popular Culture*, ed. Mark McLelland (New York: Routledge, 2017), 196–218.

28. Sukotjo, "Expression of Love," 310.

29. "KPU Bea dan Cukai Tanjung Priok Sita Ratusan Barang Ekspor dan Impor Tanpa Izin (Tanjung Priok Custom and Excise Primary Service Office Confiscated Hundreds of Export and Import Goods Without Permit)," *Detik News*, April 29, 2014, https://news.detik.com/berita/2569125/kpu-bea-dan-cukai-tanjung-priok-sita-ratusan-barang-kspor-dan-impor-tanpa-izin?hd772204btr. "Sita

Sex Toys Ilegal, Dirjen Bea Cukai: Saya Malas Pegangnya (Confiscated Illegal Sex Toys, Directorate General of Customs and Excise: I Don't Want to Touch It)," *Detik News*, December 23, 2014, https://finance.detik.com/berita-ekonomi -bisnis/d-2785663/sita-sex-toys-ilegal-dirjen-bea-cukai-saya-malas -pegangnya. Fadhil Al Birra. "Barang Porno Sitaan Bea Cukai Dimusnahkan (Porn Goods That Have Been Confiscated by Customs Will Be Destroyed)," *Jawa Pos*, August 10, 2017, https://www.jawapos.com/read/2017/08/10/150004/ barang-porno-sitaan-bea-cukai-dimusnahkan.

30. C, Twitter private message to author, my translation, November 23, 2017.

31. D, in discussion with the author, my translation, November 23, 2017.

32. Panji Islam, "Tak Layak Tonton, KPI Larang Film Anak Shin-chan (Inappropriate to Watch, Indonesian Broadcasting Commission Banned Kids Film Shin-Chan)," *Hidayatullah*, September 27, 2014, https://www.hidayatullah.com/ berita/nasional/read/2014/09/27/30384/tak-layak-tonton-kpi-larang-film -anak-shin-chan.html.

33. Buku Pintar BL, Twitter post, August 21, 2018, 10:26 PM, https://twitter.com/ BPBL_Pro/status/1031895288783331328.

34. Tricia Abigail Santos, "Uncovering Hidden Transcripts Of Resistance of Yaoi and Boys Love Fans in Indonesia, Singapore and The Philippines: Critiquing Gender and Sexual Orders Within Global Flows of Japanese Popular Culture" (PhD diss, Osaka University, 2013), https://s3.amazonaws.com/academia.edu .documents/33383381/FERMIN_-_Ph.D._Dissertation_%28Final_version%29 .pdf?AWSAccessKeyId=AKIAIWOWYYGZ2Y53UL3A&Expires=1528650017& Signature=ei9WJLA%2BYW45Smhs4dq5XCU%2BQBM%3D&response -content-disposition=inline%3B filename (accessed June 11, 2018).

35. Buku Pintar BL, Twitter post, August 21, 2018, 10:18 PM, https://twitter.com/ BPBL_Pro/status/1031893336162881536.

(Trans)Cultural Legibility and Online *Yuri!!! on Ice* Fandom

LORI MORIMOTO

Over the past decade, English language research on transnational anime fandom has proliferated in books and journals, each contribution enriching our understanding of not only the complexities of how people become transnational media fans but also the many cultural lenses far-flung fans bring to bear on Japanese popular culture. In particular, work on the transnational circulation and consumption of anime, including Mizuko Ito, Daisuke Okabe, and Izumi Tsuji's 2012 anthology, *Fandom Unbound: Otaku Culture in a Connected World*, has foregrounded the extent to which anime today at once exceeds "Japaneseness" and is emblematic of transnational media reception and fandom writ large.[1]

This essay is intended as both a contribution to such scholarship and a consideration of the transcultural implications of real-time global anime distribution and reception; that is, "the coming together of things that were previously separate[d]" by time and distance.[2] In the dark ages before the internet, anime—while often initially encountered by happenstance in video rental shops, university clubs, and the like—was often in short, secret supply outside Japan and certain South and East Asian markets. This required (would-be) fans to actively seek out the media they wanted to see, which had the ancillary effect of bolstering their fan cultural capital along axes of authenticity and esoteric knowledge. Today, overseas consumption and, in particular, fandom of anime has come to be both characterized by digital convergence and created by it as well. Simulcasts of anime series and the global reach of the sites that stream them, combined with the visible chatter they engender between rhizomatically connected fans on social media, have the potential to conduct anime far outside the imagined fandoms of corporate and government strategizing, and into fan cultural "reception communit[ies]" relatively unconcerned with dichotomies of "Japanese" and "Western."[3]

One example of such reach can be found in the transnational and transcultural reception of *Yuri!!! on Ice* (2016, hereafter *YOI*), a twelve-episode stand-alone anime broadcast during the overnight hours on TV Asahi and its affiliates, and simulcast online, with multilingual subtitles, by Youku Tudou in China and Crunchyroll.com elsewhere. It garnered 1.4 million tweets between November 24 and December 14, 2016—the highest number for the autumn anime season—and over 400 percent more tweets during the same period than second-place anime, *Haikyuu!!* (2014–16).[4] *YOI* was also named the top trending anime of 2017 on the online media fandom hub Tumblr, as calculated by tag use.[5] Moreover, to date it has amassed the fourth highest number of anime/manga-centered stories on the predominantly English-language fanfiction archive, *Archive of Our Own* (*AO3*), close behind those for the longer-running transmedia series *Haikyuu!!*, *Attack on Titan* (2013–present, *Shingeki no kyojin*) and *Naruto* (2002–17).[6] As I discuss below, given *AO3*'s strong ties to English-language (and particularly Anglo-American) media and fanfiction culture, *YOI*'s popularity there reflects its transcultural reach in intriguing ways. The decentered mélange of subjectivities that commingle in the "contact zone" of Twitter-based *YOI* fandom further suggests the inexact nature of transcultural fandom, in which language may be decoupled from nation, and cultural belongings are as likely to be found in "nonnatural" communities of affect as those of geography, race, sexuality, age, ethnicity, religion, and so on.[7]

I do not intend here to suggest that such communities are somehow free from the limitations of how they are imagined; as Bertha Chin and I have argued elsewhere, it is precisely because of disparities between how they are constituted through shared affective and *experiential* attachments and how they are imagined from both within and without, that "contact zone" encapsulates transcultural fandoms (and transculturally-situated fans) in all their sometimes-combative disarray more effectively than "community."[8] As theorized by Mary Louise Pratt, a contact zone is first and foremost a site of contestation over what may be superficially or otherwise imperfectly shared cultural practices and interpretations, "often in contexts of highly asymmetrical relations of power."[9] In the context of the intensified convergence of anime distribution channels and, in particular, global broadcasting, and the concomitant convergence of not just different fan cultures but fans whose cultural identifications may exceed the "either/or" binaries that heretofore have characterized scholarship of transnational media and its fans, "contact zone" offers enough of a remove from more structured imagined communities and their members; all with the result that we can better conceptualize both how and what happens when transcultural fandoms coalesce.

Below, I explore the ways that *YOI* works through and against generic conventions to speak to viewers with certain popular cultural repertoires outside the necessary aegis of "Japaneseness" and anime fandom, while simultaneously inhabiting a transnationally and transculturally recognizable world that both attracts and acclimates fans lacking such a repertoire. From there, I argue that *YOI* was especially culturally legible to fans active in or familiar with English-language slash culture, whose interpretative lenses raised criticisms of the show congruent with their experiences of fan–creator relations in the context of Anglo-American media. Following this, I look at how, and to whom, such criticisms were voiced on social media, with particular attention to how critical fans were imagined by the show's creators, and how closely their perceptions aligned with fans' multivaried subjectivities.

Trans/cultural Legibility in *Yuri!!! on Ice*

Yuri!!! on Ice is set in the world of international competitive figure skating and follows Katsuki Yûri, a world-class competitor who suffers from anxiety and insecurity, particularly following his poor performance at the Grand Prix Final in Sochi, Russia. When a surreptitiously filmed video of him privately skating a program made famous by Russian skating champion Victor Nikiforov goes viral, Victor takes it on himself to fly to Japan with the intention of becoming Yûri's coach. In the context of anime and manga both, the ensuing story of Yûri's progress toward the next Grand Prix Final is at once recognizable as comedic sports romance and a deft subversion of certain key tropes of the genre, a subversiveness discernible mainly by those viewers familiar enough with its Japanese popular culture surround. In particular, *YOI* rather gleefully upends generic representations of women throughout, evident especially in the character of Yûko, Yûri's childhood friend. Reunited with her following a prolonged absence from his hometown of Hasetsu, Yûri nostalgically describes her in voiceover as the "Madonna of Hasetsu Ice Castle." Indeed, her introduction through an innocently evocative glance, as well as Yûri's own reminiscences ("*Aikawarazu kawaii shi*" [And she's as cute as ever]) and self-conscious blush when she promises to "protect" (*mamoru*) him as he skates, evoke associations with other "Madonnas" of anime and manga, iconic paragons of wholesome perfection and, importantly, heterosexual first love.

Yet, this first impression is quickly and humorously dispatched when Yûri's equally generic would-be confession of love for Yûko ("*Yû-chan, boku zutto Yû-chan no koto*" [Yu-chan, I've always—]) is interrupted by the appearance of her young, singularly *unadorable* skating otaku triplets and boisterous husband (Figure 1). This is further undercut by Yûri's own childhood reminisces about Yûko and her now-husband, Takeshi, through the juxtaposition of voiceover and image: Yûri describes Yûko as his "idol" (*akogare no hito*) against a visual backdrop of his growing infatuation-from-afar with Victor, up to and including acquiring the same type of dog as Victor's pet poodle, Makkachin. When he tells Yûko that he has named the dog "Victor," she laughingly observes, "You really do like Victor, don't you?" (*Hontô ni Victor no koto ga suki nan da nê!*). The key information communicated here—that Yûri is an unreliable narrator—is legible even to those viewers outside an anime fan habitus. The moments in which we see him and Yûko gasping, wide-eyed, over Victor's programs on TV and cooing over magazine pictures of him with Makkachin are recognizable as typical fan behavior writ large. But its confounding of the generic expectations set up through the archetypical "Madonna" and Yûri's aborted love confession remains legible overwhelmingly to those fans already familiar with such conventions.

Here, it is tempting to label such fans as "Japanese" or, more broadly, "anime" fans, yet even the latter is too restrictive considered against the affordances of proximity, both geographical and virtual. At the risk of self-indulgence, I would point to my own recognition of them as one example of how such legibility is as much about such proximity as it is about (fan) community belonging. In my case, I became a fan of the Adachi Mitsuru manga

Figure 1. Screen capture of Yûri being "greeted" by his childhood friends and their kids. *Yuri!!! on Ice*, directed by Sayo Yamamoto, written by Mitsurō Kubo, aired October 5, 2016, on TV Asahi.

Touch (1981–86) while a study-abroad student in Tokyo in 1986. Ubiquitous on television, radio, and films in late 1980s Japan, *Touch* is arguably *the* quintessential sports romance (referred to in one online article as a "national" [*kokumin teki*] manga), and its female protagonist, Minami, the quintessential Madonna.[10] While familiar with, and a fan of, certain specific anime and manga works, I have neither the broad interest nor the fan cultural experience with anime and manga to call myself a fan, but rather have acquired a specific popular cultural fluency by geographical and affective happenstance. How much more, then, might the affordances of rhizomatic social media foster transcultural literacy in *certain aspects* of a given media object, and its cultural surround influence that acquisition, and to what effect?

If this subversion of generic tropes in *YOI* is legible primarily to those viewers with a particular popular cultural background, the show equally extends a welcome to viewers outside this aegis through its international characters and settings, its technologically recognizable spheres of activity, and its female characters whose desiring gaze and relative mobility invite cross-cultural identification from both women and nonbinary viewers. *YOI* is set in the world of international competitive figure skating, where annual competitions are held in major cities throughout the world, and skaters from a variety of linguistic and cultural backgrounds find themselves in relatively close quarters for a good portion of the year. Roughly half of *YOI* takes place in Yûri's Japanese hometown, and what little specific knowledge of Japan is needed to make sense of the story is seamlessly and diegetically related directly to Victor and "Yurio," another young Russian skater, further contributing to *YOI*'s transcultural accessibility. Language, too, functions somewhat fantastically to minimize cultural disjuncture not only between characters from different linguistic backgrounds, but also between text and viewers. *YOI*'s *lingua franca* is Japanese, regardless of whether the speaker is Japanese, Russian, Thai, Korean, Kazakh, and so on. When necessary (or desirable), foreignness is signified through something of a *gaijin patois*—"Amazing!" "Wow!" "Really?"—and only rarely is language tailored to a specific character (Victor's "Vkusno!"—delicious!—when trying katsudon for the first time is one such example). The practical effect of this is to essentially level the linguistic playing field for *YOI*'s characters enough to sustain affective distance and cross-cultural disjuncture between characters; an effect that similarly lowers barriers to viewers' understanding of the show, inviting them to engage intimately with it.

Moreover, familiar smartphone and laptop screens abound, and social media in particular plays a key role in Victor's decision to become Yûri's coach when, from the comfort of his St. Petersburg apartment, he sees the video of Yûri skating Victor's old program, which Yûko's triplets secretly film and upload to the internet using her smartphone (Figures 2 and 3).

We later learn through a montage of smartphone pictures that Yûri's video was only the final push needed for Victor to become his coach, a process begun

Figure 2. Screen capture of Yûko scolding her triplets for uploading the video of Yûri skating Victor's program.

Figure 3. Screen capture of Victor watching Yûri's skating.

at a banquet in which Yûri drunkenly dances with Victor before begging him to be his coach—none of which Yûri himself remembers (Figure 4).

One final point of transcultural affinity comes in the form of YOI's several female characters. As discussed above, Yûko resists symbolic co-optation as an idealized Madonna in her far more quotidian identities as employee, wife, and harried mother. But she also enjoys another moment of generic

Figure 4. Screen capture of a camera phone photo of drunken Yûri dancing with Victor after the Grand Prix Final.

Figure 5. Screen capture of Yûko's reaction to Victor's sexy skating routine.

subversiveness in her reaction to seeing Victor perform the program he has choreographed for Yûri, when the bloody nose familiar to anime and manga fans as a signifier of male heterosexual attraction spews like a fountain out of her nose (Figure 5). Indeed, rather than the object of a male gaze, women throughout *YOI* are the bearers of a specifically female fannish gaze, and men are there to look pretty, stay quiet, and fuel fantasies (Figure 6). Even Yûko's young daughters adopt a fannish gaze, albeit to more voyeuristic ends (Figure

Figure 6. Screen capture of Yûri's sister, Mari, and ballet instructor, Minako, spying on Yurio and Otabek in Barcelona.

Figure 7. Screen capture of Yûko's technology-savvy triplets.

7). The effect is to afford women fans an identificatory "in" through globally recognizable performances of female fandom. That is, the women of *Yuri!!! on Ice* are fans *like us*, a shared subjectivity that (more or less) seamlessly enfolds us in its narrative world.

Yuri!!! on Ice and Slash Fanfiction Culture

In her introduction to *Fandom Unbound: Otaku Culture in a Connected World*, Mizuko Ito observes: "The niches within the meganiche of anime are increasingly uniting fans across national boundaries. For example, the yaoi otaku fandom of Japan shares much in common with slash fandoms in the United States. Both are female-centered fandoms that center on "couplings" between male characters in popular series."[11]

While neither yaoi nor Boys' Love (BL) anime, *YOI* in fact embodies many of the characteristics (and aspirations) of English-language slash fanfiction: character pairings, or "ships" (a contraction of "relationships" popularized in *X-Files* fandom in the late 1990s), reflect certain archetypes that, while not a prerequisite for slashing two characters, translate easily across texts. As exemplified in the ur-ship of Kirk and Spock from *Star Trek* fandom, itself reflecting far more clandestine Holmes–Watson pastiche of the past, these types center on personality-based binaries of introversion/extroversion, thought/action, intellectual/physical, and shy/outgoing; they also reflect physical binaries of height and even hair color in ships ranging from Harry/Draco (*Harry Potter*), Sherlock/John (BBC *Sherlock*), Castiel/Dean (*Supernatural*), Remus/Sirius (*Harry Potter*), Bucky/Steve (*Captain America*), Loki/Thor (*Thor*), Will/Hannibal (*Hannibal*), Q/Picard (*Star Trek: The Next Generation*), Q/Bond (James Bond films featuring Ben Whishaw as Q) . . . and Yûri/Victor. *YOI's* canonical athlete/coach relationship between introverted, anxious, shy, dark-haired, (comparatively) short, and bespectacled Yûri, and extroverted, confident, outgoing, light-haired, and tall Victor is thus immediately legible within English-language slash culture.

The world of international competitive figure skating against which *YOI* is set further strengthens its legibility within slash fanfiction culture. Slash stories are overwhelmingly relationship-driven, facilitated in no small part by fans' preexisting familiarity with their narrative backdrops. As P. J. Falzone writes, in slash, "the reader does not have to ask, 'Who are these characters? Where did they come from? What is their world like?' The reader knows that from the outset," which leaves her free to dispense with "setting, background and characterization so that [she] may proceed directly to the interaction of the two protagonists."[12] Even where such world-building occurs, as in Alternate Universe (AU) stories that diverge in part or wholly from canonical events and relationships, characters typically remain sufficiently recognizable that the change in scenery remains largely undisruptive.

Historically, slash stories were based on canonical close friendships between men that were unlikely to ever evolve into fully realized romance, transformed by writers' "transgressing the borders of a parent narrative through the construction of an aberrant metatext that both ascribes to the central rule of the metatext (that otherwise heterosexual characters are queer), while refusing to break free from the parent and for its own discreet mythos."[13] Contemporary slash fanfiction has evolved away from this paradigm to a certain extent, particularly in fans' growing desires for canonical queer relationships between same-sex couples. Yet this is a complex desire, widely explained as a broader need for more and better queer representation in media on the part of both queer and straight fans, yet encompassing more normative longings for onscreen resolution of subtextual or otherwise hinted-at romance between two characters, regardless of sexual orientation.

Ultimately, however, it is the show's canonical "narrative edgeplay" that contributes most to its slash fan cultural legibility.[14] Gender transgression is the rule, rather than the exception, throughout *YOI*, reflected not only in its female characters but particularly in its visual and narrative depictions of Yûri, Victor, and a host of other male figure skaters that appear along the way. Rather than androgynous, Yûri and Victor's gender identities are explicitly coded as "both/and" through such tropes as the revealing of Victor's bare shoulder and flat chest from a slipped yukata, and the cross-gender seductiveness of his lifting Yûri's chin with long, delicate fingers to meet his eyes. Similarly, the skating costume Yûri borrows from Victor, a full-body leotard with half-skirt and spangles on one side, as well as the performance he skates following his eleventh-hour realization that he experiences the "eros" of his music more as a woman than man, is equally, if not more, "gender-blended."[15] Within the context of slash fanfiction, fans' gender play reflects what Falzone, borrowing from Freud, terms the "polysemic perversity" of slash, "a conscious return to this drive, seeking, locating, and creating outlaw pleasure outside narrative norms and copyright sanctions,"[16] involving a fundamental queering of socially sanctioned, heteronormative media texts. In the context of slash fanfiction, polysemic perversity is thus concerned not with normative notions of a gender binary and its existing limitations, but rather with "gender indifferen[ce]" as a starting point for the radical reconsideration by fans of what freedom from the constraints of "heteronormative shame-based [gender] paradigms" might make possible.[17]

Critically, the "queer" of slash here is grounded in the "perversion" of heteronormative texts and eschews "already objectified pathologies or perversions" in favor of "a horizon of possibility whose precise extent and heterogeneous scope cannot in principle be limited in advance."[18] Put differently, this understanding of queerness is by definition incompatible with today's slash fan desires for canonical queer ships, yet it continues to inform slash fans' own understanding of the fanworks they create, resulting in a constituent instability within slash fanfiction culture that paradoxically makes YOI a singularly legible text within it. Not only Falzone but Fujimoto Yukari also brings Freudian "perversity" to bear on both fan-produced and commercial yaoi and BL works. In particular, she singles out contemporary variations on a straightforward "seme-uke" (top/bottom; dominant/submissive) archetype to illustrate how the promise of polymorphic perversity of girls dressed as boys in *shôjo* (girls) manga, reflect "experiments in transgressing every possible border of sexual difference" within yaoi and BL:[19]

> A wealth of yaoi terms have come into being to describe the various relationship patterns, such as "sasoi uke" (an individual who is mentally seme but physically uke), "hetare zeme" (a loser seme), "jô uke" (a proud uke queen), "keigo zeme" (a seme who talks to his partner using honorific language), "yancha uke" (a naughty uke), or "gekokujô" (when an uke overcomes a seme). All of these terms are inherently contradictory, highlighting two different personality traits held by the same character. In an all-male world in which no biological sexual difference exists, creators of yaoi and BL make couplings by freely combining all sorts of gender factors and power dynamics as they like. Readers, for their part, are able to search for their own preferred couplings among all the possibilities offered. For both readers and creators, this is the pleasure of yaoi and BL: a thoroughly gender-blended world.[20]

YOI, with its canonical gender-blending and subversion of heteronormative sexual and gender norms, might thus be understood as embodying the polysemic/polymorphic perversity of both slash and yaoi/BL in such a way that it is uniquely legible across fan cultures.

Transcultural Legibilit(ies) in the Contact Zone

Understood in this way, what particularly intrigues me are those things that do not easily translate from one context to another within the contact zone of transcultural *YOI* fandom. This is where the habitus of slash fanfiction culture, those "generative principles of distinct and distinctive practices" that differentiate otherwise (or seemingly) congruent cultures, must be taken into consideration.[21] In the case of English-language slash fanfiction culture, we might begin with a look at two main multifandom archives of English-language fanfiction on the internet. FanFiction.net (FF.net) and *Archive of Our Own* (*AO3*) not only house fanfiction across media, languages, and national borders but also reveal something of the driving ethos of fanfiction culture, particularly where the publication of adult-themed fanfiction is concerned. FF.net, which was founded in 1998, is the largest online archive centered on English-language fanfiction, widely used by readers and writers outside an English-language environment.[22] It currently operates through money from onsite advertising, criticized by some fans as antithetical to the nonprofit "gift economy" of English-language (and particularly American) fanfiction communities going back as far as the 1970s.[23]

In contrast, *AO3* was founded in 2007 by the Organization for Transformative Works (OTW), then a collective of fans largely hailing from the early days of online fanfiction culture. This fan-run, fan-funded archive was proposed in response to two roughly coinciding upheavals within English-language fanfiction culture: the first was the 2007 attempted commercialization of fanfiction by the short-lived site FanLib.com, which teamed up with media copyright owners to host "official" fanfiction writing events that were at once extremely limited in scope and involved writers' forfeiting any rights to their work, thus enabling its commercial use. The second was what is colloquially referred to as Strikethrough2007, when the then-hub of English-language online fanfiction, *LiveJournal* (*LJ*), abruptly purged hundreds of blogs on the basis of listed "interests such as incest, rape, child pornography, and pedophilia."[24] Coming on the heels of decades of broad societal misunderstanding and censorship of adult-themed, particularly homoerotic, fanfiction, these two events were seen by many in established fanfiction communities as something of a last straw, thus prompting the establishment of *AO3*.

The differences between FF.net and *AO3* thus reflect an orientation within English language fanfiction culture that values sexual self-expression and cultural autonomy within the context of broad societal policing of female and queer sexualities on the one hand, and cooptation by corporate media on the other; each constitutive elements of an English language fanfiction cultural habitus that deeply inflects the transcultural reception and fandom of *YOI*. In turn, this habitus is what makes "different differences" between otherwise substantially congruent slash fanfiction and yaoi fan cultures that surface in the shared contact zone of transcultural *YOI* fandom.[25]

Indeed, despite the limitations of fine data collection on *AO3*, examination of *YOI* fanfiction posted to the site over the course of the series' first run begins to suggest the specific ways such differences asserted themselves among English-language slash fans of *YOI*. To give a sense of the general parameters of *YOI* fandom on *AO3*, it is worth first noting that 97 percent of *YOI* stories posted to *AO3* are written in English (although not necessarily by native English speakers), compared with only 41 percent on *FF.net*, reflecting *AO3*'s stronger ties to English language (and particularly American) fanfiction culture dating back at least as far as *LJ*. Such ties are further borne out, however circumstantially, by the high percentage of "omegaverse" stories in *YOI* fanfiction relative to the other top anime fandoms on *AO3* (Figure 8, in order of anime popularity).

"Omegaverse" is a variant of two sexual compulsion tropes popularized in early *Star Trek* fanfiction, and it historically has been endemic to English-language fanfiction; combined with *YOI*'s popularity on *AO3* relative to *FF.net* (30,000 stories versus 5,800 stories), it seems safe to say that *YOI* attracted fans from well within English-language slash culture. Working from this assumption, we find that the first *YOI* stories posted to *AO3* over the course of the series' original broadcast, by authors with no *evinced* prior experience of anime fandom, reveal certain trends that broadly correlate with the fan cultural context—that is, the cultural surround—in which they were written[26] (Figure 9). There was, in fact, one *YOI* story published on *AO3* prior to the airing of the show, with an author's note explaining, "So yeah, *Yuri!! on*

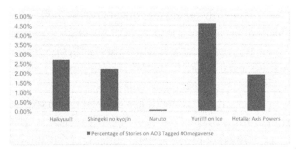

Figure 8. Percentage of anime stories on *AO3* tagged as Omegaverse by fandom.

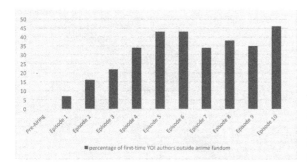

Figure 9. Percentage of first-time *YOI* fanfiction by non–anime fan authors.

Ice is an upcoming skating anime that I'm super excited for, and this is me waiting for it to come out."[27] This author, writing under three separate *AO3* pseudonyms, had also posted fanfiction for *Attack on Titan* and *Psycho Pass* (2012–13, *Saiko pasu*), as well as *ACCA: 13-Territory Inspection Dept.* (2013, *ACCA 13-ku kansatsuka*) prior to her first *YOI* story, presumably reflecting enough familiarity with online anime fandom that she would have come into contact with advertising for the series before it aired.

Such exposure to marketing seems equally true of authors posting their first *YOI* stories over the course of episodes 1 through 4, when those coming from outside anime fandom comprised less than 35 percent of the total of first-time *YOI* fanfiction posters on *AO3*. Episode 5 enjoyed a significant bump that was sustained in episode 6; however, this was followed by an equally substantial drop after episode 7 that, while difficult to ascertain with absolute certainty, appears to have been precipitated by what may, or may not, have been a kiss between Victor and Yûri. To the casual observer, these images clearly imply that a kiss has taken place. For fans of the show, what happens here is far more debatable; as one Japanese viewer tweeted: "This was so much fun! Husband: 'They're kissing!' Me: 'Nuh-uh!' [*shite hen*]" (@sima40405, December 8, 2016). Within the context of English language slash culture, this ambiguity triggered many fans' sensitivity to media "queerbaiting," itself related to those issues of sexual policing and commercial co-optation that are part and parcel of its habitus.

Joseph Brennan defines queerbaiting as a "tactic whereby media producers suggest homoerotic subtext between characters in popular television that is never intended to be actualized on screen" as a means of attracting the kinds of viewers interested in onscreen actualization of queer content encompassed within English-language slash culture; within this context, any visual and narrative ambiguity about the exact nature of a relationship perceived to be

Figure 10. Screen capture of the kiss between Victor and Yûri.

Figure 11. Screen capture of lips hidden behind an arm.

homoerotic becomes highly suspect.[28] Indeed, debates over the exact nature of the kiss that raged in parts of transcultural *YOI* fandom following episode 7 centered on the dichotomy between queerness as a signifier of open-ended gender and sexual possibility that, according to Fujimoto, similarly characterizes yaoi and BL, and queerness as a more deterministic subject position in need of greater visibility. For fans of the former interpretation, which tended to encompass those coming from a Japanese popular and fan cultural habitus, the "kiss" serves to restore some of the ambiguity important to the genre (of women-oriented anime) while still pushing the limits of genre expectations towards explicit queerness.

Never truly seen, the kiss happens without imposing a canonical interpretation of (Victor and Yûri's) relationship on the fan community that exists around the potential for a thousand kisses.[29] That is, as Caitlin Casiello suggests, in obscuring the kiss, *YOI* enabled viewers to come to their own conclusions; a perspective that in fact was reflected in *YOI* writer Kubo Mitsurou's tweeted response to fan clamoring about whether or not it was a "real" kiss: "Ultimately, I'm not saying what happened in episode 7; or, I'm not pushing an [interpretation] on anyone, so please decide for yourself."[30] Such interpretations were countered by those fans mistrustful of the broader implications of ambiguity. As Evelyn Hielkema argues:

> We are right to be suspicious of the reasons why a creator or studio might be content with teasing or suggesting rather than committing to full visibility. So the term "queerbaiting," while blunt and superficial, does hint at both the ways that all fans are exploited and the specific ways we get fetishized or mistreated in both canonical and fan works. For me, the problem is not so much how subtle or blatant the "representation" might be. Rather, the problem lies in the commodification of art and the use of LGBT people as niche fetishes and exotic subject matter by people who don't care about us or our struggles.[31]

It should be noted that the abovementioned tweet was neither the only, nor the first, tweeted by Kubo following episode 7. Posted to Twitter on the day episode 7 aired, Kubo's observation: "Is it just me, or do there seem to be similarities with this week's Nigehaji?" likens it to episode 6 of the TBS television drama, *Nigeru wa haji da ga yaku ni tatsu* (or *Nigehaji*; 2016, *The Full-Time Wife Escapist*), in which an emotionally climactic kiss occurs.[32] For fans familiar with the drama or dedicated enough to research the context of the tweet, this is all but unequivocal proof that the kiss is indeed a kiss. Nonetheless, for other fans the meaning here is either culturally opaque (one Portuguese-tweeting fan begs someone else to come translate the tweet and say if it affirms the kiss) or otherwise inaccessible, or it remains insufficient proof. As a Chilean fan writing in English tweets in response, "Kubo sensei I need confirmed the kiss! Please [three crying emoji]."[33]

Specific debate over possible queerbaiting in episode 7 was largely a fan cultural phenomenon; nonetheless, insofar as creator-side pronouncements about the nature of perceived homoeroticism can be a flashpoint of intensified debate and outcry, Kubo's tweet helped make more visible the transcultural tensions within *YOI* fandom. Suzanne Scott has argued that: "the 'bait' in queerbaiting implies *intent* on the part of media producers, with homoerotic subtext or content overtly positioned to lure LGBT audiences and/or those fans who 'see queerly'" (Kohnen 2008). Once fans are "caught" (or, more to the point, counted and sold back to advertisers), the representational bait is revealed to be something other than it initially appeared, with homoerotic desire either sublimated or foreclosed entirely."[34] If this sounds like so much fan conspiracy theory, remember that it exists against a media cultural environment in which (overwhelmingly male) Anglo-American media producers not infrequently respond to both fans' claims of homoerotic subtext in slash fiction about their work with tolerance at best, and vociferous, often patronizing, rejection at worst.

It is not uncommon for fans frustrated over perceived queerbaiting to voice their concerns on Twitter, where marketing logics often require creators and actors to have a presence that leaves them open to direct contact from fans in ways that can contribute to "the toxicity of contemporary fan/ producer relationships on social media."[35] This is the social media contact zone within which Kubo posted the above tweet, about which she recalled: "I had a huge number of reactions in my Twitter replies. For some reason, people from overseas would thank me or ask things like, "So which was it?" [laugh] But I don't want to say "Actually, it was this" and push an interpretation on anyone, and I wouldn't stop anyone from believing what they want about how things might go. [laugh] It was really interesting—Japanese people didn't ask about it at all, but foreigners came and asked outright, 'So which was it!?'"[36] Of course, both the thanks (for adequately, in some fans' minds, actualizing a kiss between men onscreen) and the questions Kubo received concerning it are legible in the context of English-language slash fan culture and its constituent concerns, and her observations about differences in what she describes as "foreign" and "Japanese" responses seem borne out in the replies to her abovementioned tweet. The small handful of English language replies, in particular, were critical of her perceived unwillingness to confirm the kiss: "be courageous. It's meant to be a kiss. Why don't you say so?"[37] and "Honestly a little bit disappointed for this. But still, thank you so much for bringing us this great story!!"[38]

It is significant that these two tweets come from outside a native English context; here, as in slash fan and fanfiction cultures themselves, English is the *lingua franca* of online communications (reflected as well in the number of *YOI* stories on *AO3* that begin with the caveat that the writer is not a native speaker of English). While this is unsurprising to anyone who has followed media tags on Twitter, what might be less expected are the two other tweets critical of Kubo. Both are in Japanese: the first from a self-described Japanese-language student who echoes the above English language replies, writing: "Would there be any reason for Yuri to be surprised by a hug from Victor? Why don't you say whether it's a kiss or not?" (@MakoHaru_matuer, December 8, 2016).³⁹ The second is a five-tweet thread by a Korean fan about how the show is, in the end, no different from queerbaiting, a discussion she links to an independent thread that explains her perspective more clearly:

> What was most important to overseas (*gaikokujin*) fans of *YOI* was whether or not this anime would stop "queerbaiting, a concept we might call fujoshi hanbai (marketing to fangirls) in Japanese, where elements of BL are included because they'll sell among fangirls, but there's no actual dating or coming about [of LGBT characters.]" When the image of what looked like a kiss appeared in episode 7, there was a huge reaction from English language [fans], who said things like, "This is the first Japanese anime to stop queerbaiting." Then, with the "ring" in today's episode 10, everyone was thrilled that there was really a 'queer protagonist' in an anime. [But] now I can't ignore Kubo-san's statement. She's saying that, in the end, she's leaving it up to your imagination whether or not the relationship between the two of them is romantic or not. So, does this mean that, in the end, the queerbaiting won't stop?⁴⁰

While this fan seems to be unfamiliar with, or uninterested in, some of the debates in English-language *YOI* fandom about whether or not the kiss was queerbaiting, she is nonetheless sufficiently conversant with English-language fan cultural habitus within which *YOI* was consumed and interpreted that she recognizes both the meaning and significance of queerbaiting to such fans. In this sense, neither Japanese nor English may necessarily be conflated with national belonging, nor are fans necessarily constrained or otherwise oriented by a discrete habitus.

Kubo notes that Japanese fans never ask her the question of whether or not the kiss was a "kiss," an observation that, in talking with fellow fans about the show, I have attributed to the legibility of certain representational tropes in *shônen* (boy's) and shôjo manga and anime (such as Adachi's aforementioned *Touch,* when the climactic kiss between protagonist Tatsuya and Minami is implied, rather than depicted, through an image of Minami's feet, tippy-toed and facing Tatsuya's). Nonetheless, Kubo's observation lends itself to the implicit assumption that Japanese fans did not think of *YOI* in those terms; and, in fact, criticism of "Western" ideas of queerbaiting being applied to *YOI* approached the issue from precisely this perspective. As one commenter notes in regards to Casiello's argument: "The discussion of 'queerbaiting' in Western English-speaking fandom is one that merits close attention. In the case of *Yuri!!! on Ice,* 'queerbaiting' imposes queerness upon the series in a way that reflects Western fans' ideals of what the purpose of the story is."[41] Similarly, another wrote, "There's definitely an undeniable difference in expectations that Western fans have in comparison to Japanese fans. The need to see explicit romantic scenes (e.g., on mouth-to-mouth contact, etc.) has Western fans quick to criticize Japanese media of 'queerbaiting,' even when that criticism is unwarranted."[42]

While both (rightly) attribute this interpretative difference to the vagaries of transcultural media reception, the notions of "Western" and "Japanese" as discrete cultural perspectives loom large here. If we consider how Kubo is approached and addressed by apparently Japanese fans on Twitter, we see a different kind of Japaneseness at work. As in the case of other well-known manga artists (of whom Kubo is one), she is addressed almost uniformly as "Kubo-sensei," reflecting a culture of respect extending at least as far back as Osamu Tezuka. While utterly ordinary within manga fan culture, considered in the context of transcultural YOI fandom, fans' use of the "sensei" suffix and the general politeness of Japanese language replies to Kubo's tweet begin to suggest that the issue might not be (just) one of "Western" approaches to "Japanese" anime, but may (also) be inflected by anime and manga fan cultural norms that eschew direct criticism of artists online.

Moreover, some discussion of queerbaiting in *YOI* did in fact take place in Japanese language posts both on Twitter and personal blogs outside the Twitter melée over the course of the show's first run, particularly among fans with ties to online queer culture.[43] As such, I want to suggest that the salient issue—here and in scholarship of present-day transcultural reception and fandom of anime generally—is less one of the intersection of discrete cultural communities, than of exactly how bordered such concepts—and the people who discuss and debate them—can be within the transcultural contact zones of online fandom.

In Lieu of a Conclusion

The observant (or critical) reader of this essay may notice the glaring absence of discussion about how *Yuri!!! on Ice* was received and understood among the viewers to whom it was ostensibly aimed. This is due in large part to space constraints, but it also reflects some of my own lack of familiarity with contemporary anime fandom in Japan. As such, the writing process throughout has been characterized by creeping worries about what this absence says about me and my presumed scholarly authority, slowing me down and effectively blinding me to the relevance of messy transcultural fan subjectivity for how we might reimagine both ourselves and how we conduct scholarly work. English-language Japanese popular culture studies historically have been characterized by their insularity; in part, I would argue, a product of the difficulty of Japanese-language acquisition for those of us outside a Sino-centric writing system, and our concomitant anxiousness to "prove" ourselves within not only our own academic structures but also academic and media industrial institutions in Japan as well. Yet this insularity is aided by a lack of engagement with recent and relevant scholarship from outside "Japan Studies," particularly where fandom is concerned. Indeed, a cursory look at several anthologies of the past decade that discuss fandom—*Fandom Unbound: Otaku Culture in A Connected World, Idols and Celebrity in Japanese Media Culture*, and *Introducing Japanese Popular Culture*—suggests that while scholars are familiar with canonical works of early fan studies and, above all, Henry Jenkins (1992), with the exception of passing citations of work by Matt Hills, Jonathan Gray (alone and with Cornel Sandvoss and C. Lee Harrington), Francesca Coppa, and Derek Johnson—no English-language scholarship of fandoms and fan cultures have been acknowledged, much less cited. Indeed, the disciplinary conservatism that sees no fewer than eleven separate citations of Henry Jenkins's work across sixteen essays echoes an equally disproportionate reliance on the work of Koichi Iwabuchi that, as Jeongmee Kim observes in the context of work on East and Southeast Asian regional television consumption, "reveals as much about critical practice as it reveals about the texts that flow throughout Asia themselves."[44]

Among the effects of such insularity is a relative dearth of collaborative work of the kind that, as it happens, characterizes transcultural grappling over meaning within online fandoms. Over the course of writing this essay, I returned repeatedly to a fan-written blog post, "That's what she said?! Kubo Mitsurou and the kiss(?)," mainly because it included the link to Kubo's abovementioned tweet, which I kept forgetting to bookmark, but also because of its nuanced interpretation of both what Kubo meant and how fans in an English-language slash cultural context interpreted it.[45] One thing in particular, however, has persisted after the writing of this essay: the blogger's confession that she would not venture into explaining something touching on debate within Japanese-language *YOI* fandom, because, "I don't know the female anime fandom in Japan all that well—one consequence of where I lived when I was there is that I was only ever able to observe it from afar."[46] She continues, "Tora has written a few posts on her own understanding of it if you're interested," with a link to the other blogger; a seemingly inconsequential move that, in the context of academic authority and single-authored scholarship, suggests to me what we are failing to take full advantage of in this convergent media moment.[47]

My research is interdisciplinary, often bringing English-language fan studies to bear on media objects and fandoms that fall outside an English-language aegis, and I am dismayed when I find scholars in Japanese studies essentially reinventing the wheel in order to discuss something that might be better grasped by adapting existing fan studies theory. There is a small-but-growing body of English-language work on Japanese popular culture consumption that engages meaningfully with fan studies scholarship as a way of drawing on the strengths of the one to better inform the other, produced in large part (and not coincidentally, I would argue) by early and mid-career women scholars. This work offers a salient model of what interdisciplinary Japanese popular culture studies might look like. As much as English-language scholarship of Japanese popular culture should engage with Japanese-language research (and it should), writ large, this essay is an attempt to demonstrate an equal imperative to step outside the disciplinary boundaries of "Japan Studies" if we are to grasp the specific contours and nuances of popular culture consumption and fandom in Japan.

···

Lori Morimoto is an independent researcher of media fandom and fan cultures. She has published essays on transnational and transcultural media fandoms in *Participations: Journal of Audience and Reception Studies*, the *East Asian Journal of Popular Culture*, and *Transformative Works and Cultures*, as well as chapters in *Fandom: Identities and Communities in a Mediated World, Second Edition*, *A Companion to Media Fandom and Fan Studies*, and *The Routledge Companion to Media Fandom*.

···

Notes

1. Ito, Mizuko, Daisuke Okabe and Izumi Tsuji, eds., *Fandom Unbound: Otaku Culture in a Networked World* (New Haven: Yale University Press, 2012).
2. Graham Meikle and Sherman Young, *Media Convergence: Networked Digital Media in Everyday Life* (New York: Palgrave Macmillan, 2012), 2.
3. Patrick Murphy and Marwan Kraidy, "Toward an Ethnographic Approach to Global Media Studies," in *Global Media Studies: Ethnographic Perspectives*, ed. Patrick Murphy and Mawran Kraidy (London: Routledge, 2003), 7.
4. "Twitter teki konki no haken anime wa? Aki anime tsuiito rankingu" (Which are the leading anime according to Twitter? Autumn anime tweet ranking), WebNewType, December 21, 2016, https://webnewtype.com/news/article/96122/ (accessed August 12, 2018).
5. "Year in Review 2017," Fandom on Tumblr, https://fandom.tumblr.com/tagged/tumblr2017 (accessed Aug 12, 2016).
6. "Fandoms," Archive of Our Own, https://archiveofourown.org/media (accessed September 10, 2012).
7. Mary Louise Pratt, "Arts of the Contact Zone," *Profession* (1991): 33–40.
8. Lori Hitchcock Morimoto and Bertha Chin, "Reimagining the Imagined Community: Online Media Fandoms in the Age of Global Convergence," in *Fandom: Identities and Communities in a Mediated World, Second Edition*, ed. Jonathan Gray, Cornel Sandvoss, C. Lee Harrington (New York: New York University Press, 2017), 174–90.
9. Pratt, "Arts of the Contact Zone," 34.
10. "Ano kokumin-teki hiroin no gendô wa 'zuzushî' 'josei toshite no amae' na no ka" (Is the behavior of that national heroine 'presumptuous' and 'self-indulgent'?), *Terebi dogach*, January 31, 2016, https://dogatch.jp/news/cx/37477/detail (accessed September 2, 2018).
11. Mizuko Ito, "Introduction," in *Fandom Unbound: Otaku Culture in a Connected World*, ed. Mizuko Ito, Daisuke Okabe, Izumi Tsuji (New Haven: Yale University Press, 2012), xix.
12. P. J. Falzone, "The Final Frontier is Queer: Aberrancy, Archetype and Audience Generated Folklore in K/S Slashfiction," *Western Folklore* 64, nos. 3-4 (2005): 253.
13. Falzone, "The Final Frontier is Queer," 253.
14. Falzone, 251.
15. Fujimoto Yukari, "The Evolution of BL as '"Playing with Gender': Viewing the Genesis and Development of BL from a Contemporary Perspective," in *Boys Love Manga and Beyond: History, Culture, and Community in Japan*, ed. Mark McLelland, Kazumi Nagaike, Katsuhiko Suganuma, James Welker, trans. Joanne Quimby (Jackson: University Press of Mississippi, 2015), 85.
16. Falzone, "The Final Frontier is Queer," 256, 258.
17. Falzone, 251.

18. David Halperin, *Saint Foucault: Towards a Gay Hagiography* (New York: Oxford University Press, 1995), 62; quoted in Falzone, 249.

19. Fujimoto, "The Evolution of BL," 85.

20. Fujimoto. 85.

21. Pierre Bourdieu, "Physical Space, Social Space, and Habitus," Vilhelm Aubert Memorial Lecture, *Report* 10 (1996), 17.

22. "FanFiction.net," Fanlore, https://fanlore.org/wiki/FanFiction.Net (accessed September 3, 2018).

23. Karen Hellekson, "A Fannish Field of Value: Online Fan Gift Culture," *Cinema Journal* 48, no. 4 (2009): 113–18.

24. "Strikethrough and Boldthrough," Fanlore.org. https://fanlore.org/wiki/Strikethrough_and_Boldthrough#cite_note-1 (accessed September 3, 2012).

25. Bourdieu, "Physical Space," 17.

26. This data was collected by hand-tabulating other media fanfiction by those YOI fanfiction authors who posted their first stories in the fandom between September 9 and December 14, 2016.

27. Velairena, "presto," Archive of Our Own, https://archiveofourown.org/works/7983583 (accessed August 23, 2018).

28. Joseph Brennan, "Queerbaiting: The 'Playful' Possibilities of Homoeroticism," *International Journal of Cultural Studies* 21, no. 2 (2016), 189.

29. Caitlin Casiello, "Gaps in the Ice: Queer Subtext and Fandom Text in *Yuri!!! on Ice*," animationstudies 2.0, https://blog.animationstudies.org/?p=1730 (accessed September 7, 2018).

30. "Kubomitsurou, "Kekkyoku wa dare ni mo oshietenai to iu ka 7 wa no koto wa dare ni mo oshitsuketenai no de jibun no handan de kimetsukete kudasai," Twitter, December 8, 2016 (accessed August 30, 2018).

31. Jacqueline Ristola, "A Roundtable on *Yuri!!! on Ice* (Part 2)," animationstudies 2.0, January 9, 2017, https://blog.animationstudies.org/?p=1809 (accessed September 7, 2018).

32. Kubomitsurou, "Konshû no nigehaji to nanka shinkuro suru mono o kanjita no wa ki no sei ka na," Twitter, November 16, 2016 (accessed August 30, 2018).

33. YumenoSekai97, "Kubo sense I need confirmed the kiss! Please [three crying emoji]," Twitter, November 19, 2016 (accessed September 10, 2018).

34. Suzanne Scott, "Towards a Theory of Producer/Fan Trolling," *Participations: Journal of Audience and Reception Studies* 15, no. 1 (2018): 149.

35. Scott, "Towards a Theory of Producer/Fan Trolling," 150.

36. "Interview with Kubo Mitsurou," *Spoon.2Di* 21 (December 2016): 26–27.

37. himeroswings, "[sad emoji] be courageous. It's meant to be a kiss. Why don't you say so?" Twitter, December 8, 2016 (accessed September 10, 2018).

38. SourCornFlakes, "Honestly a little bit disappointed for this. But still, thank you so much for bringing us this great story!!" Twitter, December 11, 2016 (accessed September 30, 2018).

39. MakoHaru_mateur, "Yûri to Vikutoru no hagu ni odoroku beki nan desu ka. Nan de kisu ka dô ka iwanain desu ka? Yappari fujoshi muke no anime nan desu ka?" Twitter, December 8, 2016 (accessed September 30, 2018).

40. sinbee_S2_yuki, "Kore wa kekkyoku 'Queerbaiting desu' to onaji imi nan desu kedo, sore shittete itte iru n desu ka? 10 wa mite sugoku kibô o motte ita n desu ga, Kubo-san ga kô itterutte koto wa sô iu imi ni shika mienai n desu kedo," Twitter, December 8, 2016 (accessed March 8, 2018).

41. Rachel C., Comment, December 27, 2016, https://blog.animationstudies.org/?p =1730 (accessed September 10, 2018).

42. Kali N., Comment, December 27, 2016, https://blog.animationstudies.org/?p= 1730 (accessed September 10, 2018).

43. For example, "Yûri!!! on aisu." matdtea, https://matdtea.exblog.jp/26255856/ (accessed September 10, 2018).

44. Jeongmee Kim, "Say *Hallyu*, Wave Goodbye: The Rise and Fall of Korean Wave Drama," in *Reading Asian Television Drama: Crossing Borders and Breaking Boundaries*, ed. Jeongmee Kim (London: I. B. Tauris, 2014), 251.

45. karice, "That's what she said?! Kubo Mitsurou and the kiss(?)," Hot Chocolate in a Bowl March 1, 2017, https://karice.wordpress.com/2017/03/01/p561/ (accessed August 23, 2018).

46. karice, "That's what she said?!."

47. karice, "That's what she said?!."